SIMPLE AIR FR_ _ _ _
COOKBOOK FOR
BEGINNERS

Quick & Easy, Budget-Friendly Recipes, With Pictures. Your Family & Friends Will Enjoy Their Favourite Roasted, Fried, Grilled and Baked Food Prepared With Your Healthy Air-Fryer.

Table of Contents

INTRODUCTION

You love fried food, but you're also faced with the trade-off of reducing guilt from all the extra fat and calories. Air frying is a fantastic alternative to deep frying. It gives you crispy breading without the excess fat.

In general, Air Fryers use a fan to circulate hot air around a cylindrical wire mesh pan. There are several types of these appliances from different brands that are designed for specific purposes, such as cooking vegetables and even making donuts.

What is an Air fryer?

An Air Fryer is basically a combi oven. This means it combines the functionality of both an oven and a toaster/grill.

Air Fryers come in two basic types: the ones that use hot air circulating around the food (hot Air Fryers) and those that use convection heat, which circulates hot grease (oil) around the food (oil-less fryers). The second type uses less oil but still gives you that nice, crispy texture. Both will taste like you've deep-fried your chicken wings or fries, without all the fat and calories.

Air Fryer cooking involves no messy pots of hot oil in your kitchen. So you may not want to use them if you are frying a lot of things. But for one or two servings, an Air Fryer beats the heat of the stove.

It's also good for people who are standing all day long in the kitchen to get fried food or snacks because it doesn't consume much space.

The Air Fryers are still relatively new, but there are already plenty of options to choose from.

Air fryers really helped me get back on track with my weight loss goals. When I started to lose some weight, I wanted to go back to eating fried food, but I didn't want the guilt that came with it.

I have been using an Air Fryer for about six months now and just love it! The chips come out really crispy! I also feel much better about eating this way because it's healthier than actual deep frying.

I love to watch the process of food turning from raw to cooked—it seems like magic. As I said, the amount of fat is much lower than in normal cooking. This item doesn't require much oil or any oil at all, and its benefit is that you can cook fast and keep the nutrients and vitamins in your food too.

I'm happy with this product, and I like it! It's pretty easy to make crispy chicken wings with this Air Fryer!

This dietary gadget turns vegetables into delicious treats; we serve Brussels sprouts fresh from the Air Fryer, which make a great side dish for poultry or meat without adding too much to your diet.

Many people complain they can't get enough air in their kitchens, and this is where the Air Fryer is ideal. It circulates hot air around food so that you don't need to add more than a quarter of the oil to your food when you fry it.

For the last two years, I've been eating less fried food and eating healthier by eating mostly salad, grilled meat, and fresh vegetables. I don't like eating my vegies steamed, but they taste great when cooked at the high temperature of a normal oven.

HOW DOES THE AIR FRYER WORK?

The Air Fryer is an appliance that works by circulating hot air around a wire mesh basket with the food inside. The hot air circulates around the food, cooking it from all sides simultaneously. The result is food similar to frying but without fat and oil.

This appliance uses infrared heat to cook the food. Infrared heat is produced by heating an element (such as your stove) that uses electrically charged particles (or ions) to heat the air around it. The air then heats the food that is placed in the basket. This method is similar to the operation of a convection oven, except that the heated air circulates around the food, rather than flowing only through it.

The difference to the oven

Air fryers are a more modern alternative to the oven. Their main difference is that they use convection currents of hot air to cook food, rather than heat from an electric coil or gas flame. This method uses less oil and often emits steam, which leaves foods more crispy on the outside while retaining moisture inside.

While electricity or gas is not needed, the only way to increase the temperature of the air in an Air Fryer is to increase the air that it pumps. Therefore, this means that if you are cooking a lot of food at once, then you will need to purchase/make a larger Air Fryer.

Air fryers are sometimes sold with accessories that can be used in conjunction with their main function. This includes shelves for extra storage space, lids for containers and cooking dishes, and even timers or alarms for when food is ready.

Benefits of Using the Air Fryer

Air fryers have steadily gained popularity among health-conscious individuals looking to step up their cooking game. And it's not hard to see why—the Air Fryer offers many benefits that far outweigh similar cooking methods.

So, what are you waiting for? Let's take a look at some of the benefits of using the air frying technique below.

1. **Faster Cooking Time**

When it comes to cooking with the Air Fryer, you get to enjoy a much faster cooking time. Since there is no oil involved in the process, there won't be any need for you to keep an eye on your food and toss it in the pan every so often to prevent it from getting burned. You'll also experience a cleaner feel in your kitchen when you use the Air Fryer since no grease splatters will occur—a fact that most dieters will appreciate!

2. **Healthier Results Compared to Frying**

Using an Air Fryer is a healthier alternative when frying is unavoidable. When using a normal frying pan, you have to use a generous amount of oil to prevent your food from sticking to the pan. While this won't be a problem for some people, it can be bad news if you're on a diet or simply try to avoid consuming too much fat.

Most people don't know that air frying involves very little oil, if any at all, depending on what dish you're preparing. This allows for healthier eating and lower-calorie meals—which is perfect for those who are on a strict diet.

3. No More Messy Oil Fires

Have you ever been frying food and suddenly been surprised by a burst out of the kitchen? If you have, then you've probably had more than one unfortunate incident where your food suddenly exploded in a pool of oil. While this might be a rare occurrence, it can still cause a fire—especially if you haven't cleaned your fryer properly.

Using an Air Fryer eliminates this problem since it doesn't require any oil to cook with. This means that there will be no burst of oil splashing on the stove or on you while you're preparing your dish. You won't have to worry about getting burned or having your kitchen catch fire from splashes of hot oil either!

4. Healthier Deep Frying Alternative

If you've never heard of the term 'deep-frying,' then here's a quick summary. Deep frying is a type of cooking technique where food is completely submerged in hot oil, resulting in a cooked exterior and a juicy interior—all without having to flip or stir the food.

This method can be dangerous since it requires you to use a lot of oil to fry your food. In fact, some frying recipes call for the use of half a cup or more of oil for each serving. However, since Air Fryers use very little oil, you don't have to worry about the dangers of getting splattered by hot oil.

5. Flavorful Results

Many people become skeptical when they hear that an Air Fryer offers great results since it doesn't require any oil to cook with. However, rest assured because the superb cooking technology used in the Air Fryers prevents your food from getting dried out or tasteless—even if you use little oil!

Disadvantages of a Hot Air Fryer

There are quite a lot of disadvantages to this type of fryer, but some are more important than others. The first is that the oil usually only lasts for a few uses, which means it should be changed sooner rather than later.

Another disadvantage is that you need to constantly monitor the temperature of your food as the Hot Air Fryer doesn't regulate itself. In addition to this, there are no other types of safety procedures that must be followed by users. The food will always be at risk of overheating.

The final disadvantage of a Hot Air Fryer is its price. This is because it costs more than a regular fryer as it needs to be on a constant heat source and there's more maintenance involved with this type of fryer. You need to regularly change the oil and clean everything out after use, which can quickly add up.

Accessories

The Cooking Oil Filter is a part that would be more suited for people who are serious about healthy eating. The filter helps remove the impurities from cooking oil before they end up in your food. It can be washed with soap and water. However, some people prefer to use warm water since greasy buildup can easily occur if it is not cleaned regularly. For best results, filters should be changed every three months. The Air Fryer accessory can also be used for filtering oil before frying fish.

The Charcoal Barbecue Filter is the type of Air Fryer accessory that not a lot of people know about. The filter is better suited for people who like to try and eat healthier and do not like the strong smells that come from non-stick pans or rubbery food. It can trap odors and thus keep your home fragrant with no distractions on your sense of smell. Moreover, it will reduce your intake of harmful chemicals on non-stick pans such as Teflon or Silverstone. Also, it can help maintain the durability of your Air Fryer.

Lift Lid is an Air Fryer accessory that eases the opening of the chamber while cooking. With the lift lid, you do not have to worry about burns on your hands or fingers when you are checking whether or not everything is ready for you to eat. The lift lid helps prevent fires by making it easier for grease and oil to drip into the shatterproof collection pan. The lift lid also helps in preventing people from using it in a way that can cause injury or damage to your home. Moreover, it allows the movement of heat away from the food being cooked, thus helping in attaining crispy food with less oil for flavor and crispiness.

The Bamboo Cutting Board is an accessory that is used to cut food. It is made out of bamboo, which is a renewable resource that can be grown in abundance. It has the look & feel of wood, but it does not absorb odors or bacteria. When bought locally, it can be used as a composting product. This makes it the perfect Air Fryer accessory for people who are trying to eat healthily and do not want to go through the hassles of cooking with non-stick pans.

A Frying Pan Cover helps protect your Air Fryer from grease and spills during cooking. It also makes the Air Fryer look more appealing. The cover is made out of heatproof material. It can be used after deep frying to prevent oil splash and sweat. Therefore, you do not have to worry about using an Air Fryer that can cause burns or injuries when it is covered with grease or oil. Just make sure that your frying pan has sufficient ventilation holes to allow the heat to escape.

Cookie sheet liners are used to keep cookies warm while they are still soft. With this Air Fryer accessory, you only need one piece of food at a time while making cookies by heating it in the air rather than using your oven die to die. The cookie sheet liner helps keep the cookies warm after being cooked. Therefore, it is best used for making layer cakes and preparing large batches of cookies at a time.

Just like any other kitchen accessory, the Air Fryer accessories can be used to help extend and enhance your cooking experience. The Air Fryer can be frustrating and tedious to use without the proper accessories that help you improve your cooking time and cooking results. We hope this list of some of the most popular accessories will help you find the perfect Air Fryer accessory for your kitchen!

How is the hot Air Fryer cleaned?

The Hot Air Fryer is easy to use and provides many options for cooking different foods. It can cook anything from eggs to pancakes, but it also can make french fries or reheat leftovers. However, some important things need to be done when using this appliance, like cleaning the fryer after every use. Here is how it's cleaned.

STEP 1:

Turn the appliance on. After starting, turn off the power. Push the power button to turn it on again. On all hot fryers, press the "Control" button once to check if it's switched to heating mode or switch off automatically after some time. If the door is opened, it will switch back on automatically, so that you can finish your meal without waiting for it to switch on again.

STEP 2:

Unplug the appliance and allow it to cool down before cleaning it manually using a soft cloth and dish soap. To avoid clogging of the fryer, do not place any wet appliances inside during cleaning or when in use.

STEP 3:

Using the same cloth, dry the inside of the fryer. Do not use heated water for drying because it can cause damage to the appliance's surface.

STEP 4:

If there are any burned or leftovers, remove them by picking them up with a spoon or spatula. Then wipe with a wet cloth to remove any remaining dirt, grease, or oil. After that, dry it again using a dry soft cloth. Avoid using sharp objects like knives or forks on stainless steel surfaces to prevent scratches and dents. Pay close attention if you intend to clean this appliance using abrasive materials like steel wool. These cleaners can also cause scratches on the surface.

STEP 5:

After cleaning the fryer, make sure that it is completely dry before closing the lid or storing it away. This will allow it to retain its original condition for longer. If there are any residual grease or oil, wipe them away using a soft cloth moistened with dish soap and water mixture. You can also use cooking spray in cleaning to prevent the splattering of oil in your kitchen. You must rinse the appliance immediately after use to avoid dirt buildup in between uses, which may cause clogging when in use in the future.

Using the hot Air Fryer is easy, but it requires proper care to preserve its structure and effectiveness. Cleaning the fryer after every use will ensure that it lasts longer and also allow you to enjoy many years of usage without repair cost.

After each use, simply wipe off any leftover food with a soft cloth. It will then retain its original quality for several years without needing repairs or replacement. You should clean up after each use so this appliance will last longer. Avoid using sharp objects to remove dirt because this may cause scratches on surfaces, especially if they are stainless steel. Also, do not place any wet or hot appliances inside if you want to avoid clogging and damage to the fryer.

Tips for Cooking in an Air-Fryer

Air fryers are all the rage these days. People love them because not only do they cook food without any oil, but they also make for a really tasty meal. But how do you make the most of your new appliance? Here are some guidelines for cooking in an Air Fryer.

- Preheat your Air Fryer to the specified temperature before adding ingredients.
- Make sure your food is placed at least one inch (2.5cm) apart; if not, it will take too long to cook and may burn or overcook outside while undercooking inside.
- Do not use metal utensils in the Air Fryer. As with any metal utensil, they will react with the hot oil and cause an off-taste.
- Avoid food that is overly greasy, either by placing it in too little oil or covering it completely while frying. Greasy food will burn quickly and become mushy before its time is up.
- While some people hate it when they flip their fried foods to brown them on the underside, others suspect that this gives the best results because the outside remains crisp, while more of the inside becomes soft and richly browned.
- Use a spatula or fork to lift foods. If you try to use a tongs, a lot of your food will end up dripping on the bottom of the Air Fryer and making a mess.
- Always check that your Air Fryer is turned off before reaching into it. Because the temperature drops quickly, turning it off is vital for safety.

Avoid these mistakes

Air Fryers are a healthy way to enjoy tasty fried foods, but they do require some attention and preparation. Here we've rounded up the most common mistakes to avoid so that your Air Fryer can continue to cook all of your favorite foods.

1. Don't overload your Air Fryer – It might sound obvious, but you'll need plenty of room for food inside the basket. So if you're cooking two large potatoes and four chicken breasts, try using two batches instead of one.
2. You don't want to overcrowd the oil, which can cause splattering and having to re-fry multiple batches.
3. Use the right amount of oil – Once you've worked out how many potatoes, chicken breasts, or eggs you need, then it's time to put the right amount of oil in. It should be enough so that your food slides around freely but not so much that it overflows.
4. Measure correctly – It's important to use the correct amounts of salt and seasonings, otherwise, you'll end up irritated with your food. To measure correctly, fill a measuring jug halfway with boiling water and then fill that up with ice-cold water. The level should be halfway between the marks for salt and pepper.
5. Don't forget your fats and spices – Some people like to add a bit of oil to their food, if it's very lean, such as fish or vegetables. You can also use this time to add any spices you might want to include.

6. Don't leave your food in too long – As soon as the end of the timer beeps (and it will beep, and keep beeping until you lift the basket out), lift your food out straight away and serve straight away or put it into a preheated oven for further cooking. Never leave anything cooking in the fryer after the cycle has finished.

AIR FRYER TIPS & TRICKS

Air fryers are all about convenience, speed, and simplicity. That's why we've compiled some super easy-to-follow Air Fryer tips and tricks to help you get the most out of your appliance. You can enjoy crispy fried foods without any of the bad stuff like fat or grease! So if you're ready to save money, time, and enjoy delicious food guilt-free, read on for tips on how to prepare meals using your Air Fryer.

Keep in mind you might need to adjust the cooking time depending on the size of your food—and yes, for meats, which tend to be slower than vegetables, you'll need to break down the preparation process into two or three stages.

20 Tips and Tricks

1. To dice onions and other vegetables, we recommend using a mandolin slicer with a fine blade. A food processor works fine as long as you don't over-process or puree them.
2. Cut the core out of potatoes, wash them, and slice them in half. Cook them on both sides in the Air Fryer basket—the cooking time will depend on how crispy you want them. If you're unsure, start very low (5 minutes) and increase the time if needed.
3. When cooking meats, make sure they are dry before putting them in the basket. If you're using a marinade or sauce, place it in a pan and cook it until it thickens to avoid your meat from getting dry. Make sure to cover it so it doesn't splatter and damage your Air Fryer.
4. Always thaw meat and fish before putting them in the basket—and make sure they're completely defrosted. You can place them in the basket frozen, but you'll need to adjust the cooking time accordingly (double it).
5. 5 – When deep-frying foods, use a thermometer to make sure the oil stays at 350-360 °F (170-180 °C) . Note that vegetable oil has a lower smoke point than other oils, so as soon as you notice the oil sputtering and smoking, it's time to empty the basket and let the oil cool down. When re-using the oil, make sure it doesn't burn or smoke again. Most Air Fryers come with a defrost mode where you can use low heat and not exceed 350 °F (170 °C) .
6. If you're cooking frozen foods on high heat, adjust the temperature. Adjust the knob to 350-360 °F (170-180 °C) with the convection airflow on and the remaining three baskets on high. You can also use those baskets as a stir fry or as a base for other cooking methods.
7. An essential tip with any appliance is to keep it clean. If you don't keep it clean, food particles and grease will accumulate. For this reason, we recommend using an oil mister or brush to maintain your fryer's condition and make sure there are no areas that need cleaning.
8. When cleaning your Air Fryer, use warm water with dish soap. Avoid strong cleaning products as they can damage the enamel coating inside the basket.
9. Wash all removable parts of your Air Fryer. While it's not necessary to fill the basket completely to clean it, you should take out any residue using a soft brush or sponge—especially near the heating elements. You should also wash any removable parts of the Air Fryer—the drip tray, the oil well, and other accessories—to avoid grease build-up and food particles falling into critical areas of your appliance.
10. Air fryers are high-tech machines, so if you need to clean them, make sure to open them up. If you can't open it, remove the basket and its removable parts. Using warm water with dish soap, clean the inside of the basket. Using a soft brush or sponge, remove any residue using a gentle scrubbing motion.

11. If your Air Fryer is stained or dirty from food particles, wash it with warm water and one tablespoon of vinegar. Scrub discreetly around the heating elements with a soft brush or sponge before rinsing with cool water—don't immerse the basket below the water line.

12. To clean the outside of your Air Fryer, wipe it with a damp cloth and warm water. Don't use soap or detergent, as they can discolor or damage the finish.

13. Never reach inside an operating Air Fryer, even if you're using gloves! If you need to get something out of your basket, use oven mitts—and don't let any part of your body touch the basket while it's operating. When removing food from the basket, avoid sliding it with your fingers or using any metal utensils—make sure to remove it with oven mitts.

14. Be sure to use high-quality cooking oil for deep frying, as it will make a difference in the taste and texture of your food.

15. If you want to avoid hot spots on your basket, turn the basket every 15-20 minutes while food is cooking. Do this by using a pair of tongs or oven mitts.

16. When seasoning your basket, fry minced onion. It will coat the basket with a light layer of oil that will keep food from sticking to it.

17. When using the rack, never put anything on the top—it will get too hot. Also, avoid putting things with edges on the bottom of the basket—for example, peppers or melons—as they will roll-off. Put your food on it in an even layer with thicker items at the bottom.

18. Never use metal utensils when you're cooking with your Air Fryer. As it heats up, it can cause heavy scratches and dents on your appliance. Instead of metal utensils, use silicone or wooden utensils for optimal safety and longevity of your Air Fryer's finish.

19. Don't overwork food in the Air Fryer. It will only heat up and release moisture instead of quickly crisping it.

20. When using a drip tray, fill it with a layer of oil that is ⅛-inch thick—just enough to block any splatters from impacting your Air Fryer's finish. If you don't use a drip tray, make sure to keep an eye on any splatters—they can damage the outside of your appliance.

APPETIZERS AND SNACKS RECIPES

APPETIZERS AND SNACKS

1. Mayo Tortellini Appetizer

 10 min.   10 min.

 20 mins   4-5

- ½ c. flour
- ½ teaspoon dried oregano
- 1 ½ cups breadcrumbs
- ¾ c. mayonnaise
- 2 tablespoons mustard
- 1 egg
- 2 tbsp. olive oil
- 2 cups cheese tortellini, frozen

1. Place your Air Fryer on a flat kitchen surface; plug it and turn it on. Set temperature to 355 °F (180 °C) and let it preheat for 4-5 minutes.
2. In a bowl of medium size, thoroughly mix the mayonnaise and mustard. Set aside. In a bowl of medium size, thoroughly whisk the egg.

3. In another bowl, combine the flour and oregano. In another bowl, combine the breadcrumbs and olive oil.
4. Take the tortellini and add to the egg mixture, then into the flour, then into the egg again. Lastly, add the breadcrumbs to coat well.
5. Add the tortellini to the basket. Push the air-frying basket in the Air Fryer. Cook for 10 minutes until turn golden.
6. Slide-out the basket; serve with the mayonnaise.

 Cal: 542kcal | Carb: 26.3g | Fat: 28.6g | Prot: 18g | Fiber 3.6g

2. Eggs Spinach Side

 5 min.   12 min.

 17 mins   2-3

- 1 medium-sized tomato, chopped

- 1 tsp. lemon juice
- ½ tsp. coarse salt
- 2 tbsp. olive oil
- 4 eggs, whisked
- 5 oz. (140 g) spinach, chopped
- ½ tsp. black pepper
- ½ c. basil, roughly chopped

1. Place your Air Fryer on a flat kitchen surface; plug it and turn it on. Set temperature to 280 °F (140 °C) and let it preheat for 4-5 minutes.
2. Take out the air-frying basket and gently coat it using the olive oil.
3. In a bowl of medium size, thoroughly mix the ingredients except for the basil leaves.
4. Add the mixture to the basket. Push the air-frying basket in the Air Fryer. Cook for 10-12 minutes.
5. Slide-out the basket; top with basil and serve warm with sour cream!

Cal: 272kcal | Carb: 5.4g | Fat: 23g | Prot: 13.2g | Fiber 2g

3. **Crispy Cauliflower Bites**

 5 minutes   15 minutes

 20 mins   4

- 1 tbsp. Italian seasoning
- 1 c. flour
- 1 c. milk
- 1 egg, beaten
- 1 head cauliflower, cut into florets

1. Preheat the Air Fryer to 390 °F (200 °C) . Using cooking spray, coat the Air Fryer basket. Combine the flour, milk, egg, and Italian spice in a mixing bowl.
2. Drain the excess liquid after coating the cauliflower in the mixture.
3. Spray the florets w/ cooking spray and Air Fry them for 7 minutes.
4. Continue to cook for another 5 minutes after shaking. Allow time for the dish to cool before serving.

Cal: 70kcal | Carb: 2g | Fat: 1g | Prot: 3g

4. **Air-Fried Chicken Thighs**

5 minutes 15 minutes

 20 mins 4

- 1 ½ lb. chicken thighs
- 2 eggs, lightly beaten
- 1 c. seasoned breadcrumbs
- ½ tsp. oregano
- Salt and black pepper, to taste

1. Preheat the Air Fryer to 390 °F (200 °C). Oregano, salt, and pepper are used to season the chicken. Add the beaten eggs to a mixing dish. Place the breadcrumbs in a separate bowl. After dipping the chicken thighs in the egg wash, roll them in the breadcrumbs and press firmly to ensure that the breadcrumbs adhere properly.
2. Spray the chicken with cooking spray and place it in a single layer, skin-side up, on the frying basket. Cook for 12 minutes in the Air Fryer, then flip the chicken thighs and cook for another 6-8 minutes. Serve.

Cal: 190kcal | Carb: 11g | Fat: 8g | Prot: 16g

5. <u>Balsamic zucchini slices</u>

 5 minutes 50 minutes

 55 mins 6

- 3 zucchinis, thinly sliced
- Salt and black pepper to taste
- 2 tablespoons avocado oil
- 2 tablespoons balsamic vinegar

1. Mix all the ingredients.
2. Put the zucchini mixture in your Air Fryer's basket and cook at 220 ° f for 50 minutes.
3. Serve as a snack and enjoy!

 Cal: 40kcal | Carb: 14g | Fat: 4g | Prot: 6g | Fiber 2g

6. **Turmeric carrot chips**

 5 minutes   25 minutes

 30 mins   4

- 4 carrots, thinly sliced
- Salt and black pepper to taste
- ½ teaspoon turmeric powder
- ½ teaspoon chat masala
- 1 teaspoon olive oil

1. Put the ingredients in a bowl to toss.
2. Put the mixture in your Air Fryer's basket and cook at 370 °F (190 °C) for 25 minutes, shaking the fryer from time to time.
3. Serve as a snack.

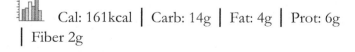 Cal: 161kcal | Carb: 14g | Fat: 4g | Prot: 6g | Fiber 2g

7. **Lentils snack**

 5 minutes   12 minutes

 17 mins   4

- 15 ounces canned lentils, drained
- ½ teaspoon cumin, ground
- 1 tablespoon olive oil
- 1 teaspoon sweet paprika
- Salt and black pepper to taste

1. Mix all the ingredients.
2. Transfer the mixture to your Air Fryer and cook at 400 °F (200 °C) for 12 minutes.
3. Divide into bowls and serve as a snack or a side, or appetizer!

 Cal: 151kcal | Carb: 14g | Fat: 4g | Prot: 6g | Fiber 2g

8. <u>Salmon tarts</u>

 20 min   10 minutes

 30 mins   15

- 15 mini tart cases
- 4 eggs, lightly beaten
- ½ c. heavy cream
- Salt and black pepper
- 3 oz. (85 g) smoked salmon
- 6 oz. (170 g) cream cheese, divided into 15 pieces
- 6 fresh dill

1. Mix together eggs and cream in a pourable measuring container. Arrange the tarts into the Air Fryer. Pour in the mixture into the tarts, about halfway up the side, and top with a piece of salmon and a piece of cheese. Cook for 10 minutes at 340 °F (170 °C) , regularly check to avoid overcooking. Sprinkle dill and serve chilled.

 Cal: 415kcal │ Carb: 2g │ Fat: 4g │ Prot: 14g

9. <u>Bacon & chicken wrapped jalapenos</u>

 40 min   30 minutes

 1 h and 10 mins   4

- Jalapeno peppers, halved lengthwise and seeded
- 4 chicken breasts, butterflied and halved
- 6 oz. (170 g) cream cheese
- 6 oz. (170 g) cheddar cheese
- 16 slices bacon
- 1 c. breadcrumbs
- Salt and pepper to taste
- 2 eggs
- Cooking spray

1. Season the chicken on both sides. In a bowl, add cream cheese, cheddar, a pinch of pepper, and salt. Mix well.
2. Take each jalapeno and spoon in the cheese mixture to the brim. On a working board, flatten each piece of chicken and lay 2 bacon slices each on them.

3. Place a stuffed jalapeno on each laid-out chicken and bacon set and wrap the jalapenos in them.
4. Preheat the Air Fryer to 350 °F (180 °C) . add the eggs to a bowl and pour the breadcrumbs into another bowl. Also, set a flat plate aside.
5. Take each wrapped jalapeno and dip it into the eggs and then in the breadcrumbs. Place them on the flat plate.
6. Lightly grease the fryer basket with cooking spray. Arrange 45 breaded jalapenos in the basket and cook for 7 minutes.
7. Once the timer beeps, open the fryer, turn the jalapenos, and cook further for 4 minutes.
8. Once ready, remove them onto a paper towel-lined plate. Repeat the cooking process for the remaining jalapenos.
9. Serve with a sweet dip for an enhanced taste.

Cal: 192kcal | Carb: 14g | Fat: 4g | Prot: 6g | Fiber 2g

10. <u>Chicken with Herbs and Cream</u>

 5 to 10 minutes   15 minutes

 20 mins   4

- 4 ounces garlic and herb cream cheese
- Salt and pepper to taste
- 2 teaspoons dried Italian seasoning
- Olive oil as needed
- 2 chicken breast fillets

1. Take the chicken and brush them with oil
2. Season them with salt, pepper, and Italian seasoning
3. Top them with garlic and herb cream cheese
4. Roll up the chicken carefully
5. Transfer them to the Air fryer basket
6. Place the basket inside the appliance
7. AIR fry for 7 minutes per side, at 370 °F (190 °C)
8. Serve and enjoy!

Cal: 750kcal | Carb: 20g | Fat: 42g | Prot: 73g | Saturated Fat 10g | Saturated Fat 18g | Fiber 3g | Sodium 846mg

11. <u>Meaty Bratwursts</u>

5 to 10 minutes   12 minutes

 17 mins   4

- 1 pack bratwursts

1. Preheat your Air Fryer in AIR CRISP mode for 5 minutes at 350 °F (180 °C)
2. Add bratwurst to the Cooking basket
3. Cook for 10 minutes, flip once.
4. Enjoy!

Cal: 739kcal | Carb: 13g | Fat: 57g | Prot: 37g | Saturated Fat 20g | Fiber 3g | Sodium 2641mg

12. **Delicious Taco Cups**

 5 to 10 minutes   10 minutes

 15 mins   4

- 1 c. cheddar cheese, shredded
- 2 tablespoons taco seasoning

- ½ c. tomatoes, chopped
- 1-pound (450 g) ground beef, cooked
- 12 wonton wrappers

1. Press wrappers firmly onto the muffin pan
2. Transfer the pan inside your Air Fryer
3. Air Fry on AIR CRISP mode for 5 minutes at 400 °F (200 °C)
4. Top with ground beef and tomatoes,
5. Sprinkle taco seasoning, cheese
6. Air Fry for 5 minutes more
7. Enjoy!

Cal: 431kcal | Carb: 29.5g | Fat: 21g | Prot: 31g | Saturated Fat 7g | Saturated Fat 30g | Fiber 5g | Sodium 604mg

13. **Mustard and Vegie**

 5 to 10 minutes   30 to 40 minutes

 35 mins   4

Vinaigrette

- ½ c. olive oil
- ½ c. avocado oil

- ¼ teaspoon pepper
- 1 teaspoon salt
- 2 tablespoons honey
- ½ c. red wine vinegar
- 2 tablespoons Dijon vinegar

Vegies

- 4 zucchinis, halved
- 4 sweet onion, quartered
- 4 red pepper, seeded and halved
- 2 bunch green onions, trimmed
- 4 yellow squash, cut in half

1. Take a small bowl and whisk in mustard, honey, vinegar, salt, and pepper. Add oil and mix well
2. Set Air Fryer to 10 minutes
3. Transfer onion quarter to Grill Grate, cook for 5 minutes
4. Flip and cook for 5 minutes more
5. Grill remaining veggies in the same way, giving 7 minutes per side for zucchini and 1 minute for green onions
6. Serve with mustard vinaigrette on top
7. Enjoy!

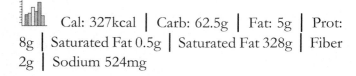 Cal: 327kcal | Carb: 62.5g | Fat: 5g | Prot: 8g | Saturated Fat 0.5g | Saturated Fat 328g | Fiber 2g | Sodium 524mg

14. <u>**Homemade Fries**</u>

 15 minutes   45 minutes

 1 h and 0 min

- 1 lb. large potatoes, sliced into strips
- 2 tablespoons vegetable oil
- Salt to taste

1. Toss potato strips in oil.
2. Add crisper plate to the Air Fryer basket.
3. Choose air fry function. Set it to 390 °F (200 °C) for 3 minutes.
4. Press start to preheat.
5. Add potato strips to the crisper plate.
6. Cook for 25 minutes.
7. Stir and cook for another 20 minutes.

Cal: 183kcal | Carb: 5.4g | Fat: 7.4g | Prot: 22.3g | Fiber 1g

15. <u>Zucchini Strips with Marinara Dip</u>

 1 Hour and 10 minutes 30 minutes

 40 mins 8

- 2 zucchinis, sliced into strips
- Salt to taste
- 1 ½ cups all-purpose flour
- 2 eggs, beaten
- 2 cups bread crumbs
- 2 teaspoons onion powder
- 1 tablespoon garlic powder
- ¼ cup Parmesan cheese, grated
- ½ cup marinara sauce

1. Season zucchini with salt.
2. Let sit for 15 minutes.
3. Pat dry with paper towels.
4. Add flour to a bowl.
5. Add eggs to another bowl.
6. Mix remaining ingredients except for marinara sauce in a third bowl.
7. Dip zucchini strips in the first, second, and third bowls.
8. Cover with foil and freeze for 45 minutes.
9. Add crisper plate to the Air Fryer basket.
10. Select the air fry function.
11. Preheat to 360 °F (180 °C) for 3 minutes.
12. Add zucchini strips to the crisper plate.
13. Air fry for 20 minutes.
14. Flip and cook for another 10 minutes.
15. Serve with marinara dip.

Cal: 364kcal | Carb: 8g | Fat: 0g | Prot: 8g | Saturated Fat 17g | Fiber 1.5g | Sodium 291mg

16. <u>Parmesan Cabbage Wedges</u>

 5 minutes 20 minutes

 25 mins 4

- ½ a head cabbage
- 2 cups parmesan
- Four tablespoons melted butter
- Salt and pepper to taste

1. Preheat your Air Fryer to 380 °F (190 °C) .
2. Take a container and add melted butter, and season with salt and pepper.

3. Cover cabbages with your melted butter.
4. Coat cabbages with parmesan.
5. Transfer the coated cabbages to your Air Fryer and bake for 20 minutes.
6. Serve with cheesy sauce and enjoy!

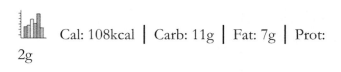 Cal: 108kcal | Carb: 11g | Fat: 7g | Prot: 2g

BREAKFAST

17. Roasted Potato wedges

 10 minutes   10 minutes

 20 mins   6

- 2 lbs. potatoes, cut into wedges
- 2 tbsp. McCormick's chipotle seasoning
- ¼ c. olive oil

1. Add potato wedges into the mixing bowl.
2. Add remaining ingredients over potato wedges and toss until well coated.
3. Transfer potato wedges onto the Air Fryer oven tray roast at 400 °F (200 °C) for 5 minutes.
4. Turn potato wedges to the other side and roast for 5 minutes more.

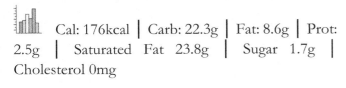 Cal: 176kcal | Carb: 22.3g | Fat: 8.6g | Prot: 2.5g | Saturated Fat 23.8g | Sugar 1.7g | Cholesterol 0mg

18. Coated Avocado Tacos

 10 minutes   20 minutes

 30 mins   12

- 1 avocado
- 1 egg
- ½ c. panko breadcrumbs
- Salt
- Tortillas and toppings

1. Take avocados and scoop out the meat from each avocado shell and slice them into wedges
2. Beat the egg in a shallow bowl
3. Put the breadcrumb in another bowl
4. Dip the avocado wedges in the beaten egg and coat with bread crumbs
5. Sprinkle them with a bit of salt
6. Take a cooking basket and arrange them in a single layer

7. In the Air Fryer cook for 15 minutes at 392 °F (200 °C)
8. Shake the basket after 10 minutes

 Cal: 179kcal | Carb: 26.3g | Fat: 6.1g | Prot: 4.9g

19. Spiced Sweet Potato Fries

 10 minutes   35 minutes

 45 mins   2

- 1 sweet potato
- 1 teaspoon parmesan cheese, grated
- ½ teaspoon cajun seasoning
- 1 tablespoon extra-virgin olive oil
- ½ teaspoon salt

1. Slice the sweet potato into ¼ inch thick sticks
2. Take a bowl and put the potatoes
3. Add remaining ingredients and toss until coated
4. Put half of the fries in the cooking basket
Cook for 10 minutes at 400 °F (200 °C) in the Air Fryer

 Cal: 131kcal | Carb: 22g | Fat: 13.8g | Prot: 1g

20. Crispy Potato Skins

 5 minutes   55 minutes

 1 h and 0 min   2

- 2 Yukon Gold potatoes
- 4 bacon strips
- 2 green onions, minced
- ¼ c. cheddar cheese, shredded
- 1/3 c. sour cream
- ½ teaspoon olive oil
- ¼ teaspoon of sea salt

1. Rinse and scrub the potatoes to clean
2. Rub with oil and sprinkle with salt
3. Put them in the cooking basket
4. Cook for 5 mins at 400 °F (200 °C) in the Air Fryer
5. Take a plate and transfer it and crumble into bits

6. Slice the potatoes into half and scoop out most of the meat
7. Arrange the potato skin with the skin facing side up in the cooking basket
8. Spray them with oil
9. Cook for 3 mins at 400 °F (200 °C)
10. Then flip the potato skins
11. Fill each piece with cheese and crumbled bacon
12. Cooking 2 minutes more

 Cal: 483kcal | Carb: 92.8g | Fat: 8.7g | Prot: 12.5g

1. Take a bowl & combine all the ingredients
2. Let them leave for 20 minutes to marinate
3. Toss the mixture several times during the process
4. Arrange half of the potato wedges in the cooking basket of the Air Fryer
5. Cook for 9 mins at 400 °F (200 °C)
6. Then toss the potato wedges and cook for 3 minutes, then cook the remaining potato

 Cal: 110kcal | Carb: 1.1g | Fat: 11.7g | Prot: 0.3g

21. <u>**Air Fryer Potato Wedges**</u>

 10 minutes   40 minutes

 50 mins   4

- 4 Yukon gold potatoes
- ½ c. extra-virgin olive oil
- 1 rosemary spring, chopped
- 3 garlic cloves
- ¼ teaspoon cayenne pepper
- 1 teaspoon of sea salt
- 1 teaspoon lemon juice

22. <u>**Coated Onion Rings**</u>

 5 minutes   10 minutes

 15 mins   2

- 2 flax eggs, whisked (or eggs substitute)
- ½ teaspoon cinnamon powder
- 2 large onion, sliced
- ½ c. breadcrumbs
- ¼ teaspoon salt
- ¼ teaspoon black pepper

- ½ c. of corn flour

1. Preheat Air Fryer to 370 °F (190 °C)
2. Take a bowl and add cinnamon powder, black pepper, flour, and salt
3. Mix them well
4. Dip each onion ring into eggs then roll out into a flour mixture
5. Dip ring again into egg then roll out into breadcrumbs
6. Place onion rings into the Air Fryer and cook for 5 minutes
7. Now flip and cook for more than 5 minutes

Cal: 169kcal │ Carb: 9.3g │ Fat: 6.4g │ Prot: 3.4g

23. Balsamic-Glazed Cool Carrots

 5 minutes   18 minutes

 23 mins   4

- 3 medium carrots
- 1 tablespoon orange juice

- 2 teaspoons balsamic vinegar
- 1 teaspoon olive oil
- 1 teaspoon maple syrup
- ½ teaspoon dried rosemary
- ¼ teaspoon salt
- ½ teaspoon lemon zest

1. Preheat your Air Fryer to 392 °F (200 °C)
2. Trim ends of carrots, cut into spears of 2 inches (5,1 cm) long
3. Transfer carrots to Air fryer and add orange juice, balsamic vinegar, maple syrup, rosemary, salt and zest
4. Stir well
5. Transfer baking dish to your Air Fryer and cook for 4 minutes, stir and cook for 5 minutes more
6. Stir & cook for 4 minutes more until carrots are nicely glazed and cooked

Cal: 48kcal │ Carb: 8g │ Fat: 2g │ Prot: 1g

24. Crazy Green Tomatoes

 8 minutes   15 minutes

 23 mins   4

- ¾ c. cornmeal
- 2 tablespoons chickpea flour
- 1 teaspoon seasoned salt
- 1 teaspoon onion granules
- ¼ teaspoon fresh ground black pepper
- ½ c. almond milk
- 2 large green tomatoes, cut into ¼ inch rounds

1. Preheat your Air Fryer to 392 °F (200 °C)
2. Take a medium-sized bowl and add cornmeal, flour, salt, onion, and pepper, stir well
3. Take another bowl and add milk, keep it on the side
4. Dip each tomato slice in milk, then coat lightly with cornmeal mixture
5. Transfer to preheated Air Fryer and cook for 6 minutes
6. Remove them and spray tops with a bit of oil, transfer back to the fryer and cook for 3 minutes, flip & cook for 3-6 minutes more until crispy

 Cal: 168kcal | Carb: 32g | Fat: 2g | Prot: 5g

25. **Rosemary Flavored Potato Chips**

 5 minutes   12 minutes

 17 mins   4

- Cooking oil as needed
- 1 small-medium sweet potato, thinly sliced
- ¼ teaspoon dried rosemary
- Dash of salt

1. Preheat your Air Fryer to 392 °F (200 °C)
2. Grease the Air Fryer cooking basket with oil, transfer sweet potatoes to the basket, and spray oil on top
3. Sprinkle salt and rosemary, cook for 4 minutes
4. Shake basket and cook for 4 minutes more

 Cal: 93kcal | Carb: 21g | Fat: 1g | Prot: 2g

26. Cheesed Up Vegan Fries and Shallots

 15 minutes 15 minutes

 30 mins 4

- Cooking oil as needed
- 1 large potato, cut into ¼ inch thick slices
- 1 teaspoon coconut oil
- ¼ teaspoon salt
- ⅛ teaspoon ground black pepper
- 1 large shallot, thinly sliced
- ½ c. + 2 tablespoons vegan cheese/cashew cheese
- 2 tablespoons chives/scallions, minced

1. Preheat your Air Fryer to 392 °F (200 °C)
2. Take a medium-sized bowl and add potato slices with salt, oil, and pepper
3. Transfer to Air Fryer cooking basket, cook for 6 minutes, shake and cook for 4 minutes more
4. Remove and add shallots, fry for 5 minutes
5. Shake basket once more and cook for 4 minutes more until they are crispy

6. Serve with a top of cashew/vegan cheese with a sprinkle of chives and scallions

 Cal: 189kcal │ Carb: 29g │ Fat: 5g │ Prot: 7g

27. Cool Berber Spiced Fries

 5-10 minutes 20 minutes

 25 mins 4

- 1 large potato, 3/4 pound (340 g) s
- 1 tablespoon sunflower oil
- 1 teaspoon coconut sugar
- 1 teaspoon garlic granules
- ½ teaspoon berbere
- ½ teaspoon salt
- ¼ teaspoon turmeric
- ¼ teaspoon paprika
- Cooking oil spray as needed

1. Preheat your Air Fryer to 392 °F (200 °C)
2. Scrub potatoes and cut them into French Fry shapes
3. Spray cooking basket with cooking oil

4. Take a medium bowl and add potato pieces, oil, sugar, garlic, berbere, salt, turmeric, paprika, and stir well
5. Transfer to Air Fryer and cook for 8 minutes
6. Shake and cook for 8 minutes more
7. Stir and cook for 3-5 minutes more browned well

 Cal: 205kcal | Carb: 32g | Fat: 8g | Prot: 4g

28. <u>**Miso Brussels**</u>

 8 minutes   11 minutes

 19 mins   4

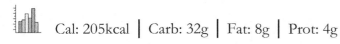

- Cooking oil spray as needed
- 2 and ½ cups Brussels, trimmed
- 1 and ½ tablespoons maple syrup
- 1 and ½ teaspoons mellow white miso
- 1 teaspoon toasted sesame oil
- 1 teaspoon tamari
- 2 large garlic cloves, minced
- 1 teaspoon fresh ginger, grated
- ¼ teaspoon red chili flakes

1. Preheat your Air Fryer to 392 °F (200 °C)
2. Spray cooking basket with cooking oil
3. Add trimmed Brussels to your Air Fryer cooking basket, cook for 6 minutes, shake and spray oil. Cook for 5 mins more until they are crispy and browned
4. Take a medium bowl and add maple syrup and miso, whisk well until smooth
5. Add sesame oil, 1 teaspoon tamari, garlic, ginger, chili flakes, and stir
6. Add Brussels to the bowl and stir well

 Cal: 67kcal | Carb: 12g | Fat: 2g | Prot: 2g

29. <u>**Spiced Up Okra**</u>

 8 minutes   20 minutes

 28 mins   4

- ½ lb. okra
- 1 tablespoon coconut oil, melted
- 1 teaspoon cumin
- 1 teaspoon coriander
- 1 teaspoon garlic granules

- ¼ teaspoon salt
- ¼ teaspoon turmeric
- ¼ teaspoon cayenne
- 1 teaspoon fresh lime juice

1. Preheat your Air Fryer to 392 °F (200 °C)
2. Take a medium bowl and add okra and toss with oil
3. Add cumin, coriander, garlic, salt, turmeric, cayenne, and stir well
4. Transfer okra to Air Fryer cooking basket and cook for 7 minutes
5. Shake the basket and cook for 7 minutes more, check for doneness, and cook for 6 minutes more if needed
6. Once the okra's feel crispy, they are ready
7. Sprinkle lime juice on top and serve

 Cal: 67kcal | Carb: 12g | Fat: 2g | Prot: 2g

30. **Blooming Onion**

 15 minutes   10 minutes

 25 mins   1

- 2 Flax-Eggs
- 4 tsp. old bay seasoning
- 1 large onion
- 2 ½ cups almond flour
- ½ c. of coconut milk

1. Slice the top of onion while keeping its base intact
2. Wash it thoroughly & drain all the water out of it
3. Carve several slits vertically from top to bottom at an equal distance
4. You must cut up to 1 inch above the base
5. Spread the onion layers like flower petals and set them aside
6. Set the Air Fryer to 400 °F (200 °C)
7. Whisk eggs with milk in one bowl and mix flour with seasoning in another
8. Dip it in the egg mixture
9. Sprinkle the remaining flour mixture over it and shake off the basket to the fryer
10. Air fry for 10 minutes

Cal: 158kcal | Carb: 10.4g | Fat: 10.6g | Prot: 6.6g

31. **Bacon Brussels Sprouts**

10 minutes   30 minutes

 40 mins   4

- 1 lb. brussels sprouts, cut into half
- ½ avocado, diced
- ¼ cup onion, sliced
- 4 bacon slices, cut into pieces
- 1 tsp. garlic powder
- 3 tbsp. lemon juice
- 2 tbsp. balsamic vinegar
- 3 tbsp. olive oil
- Pepper
- Salt

1. In a small bowl, whisk together oil, garlic powder, 2 tbsp. lemon juice, and salt.
2. In a mixing bowl, toss brussels sprouts with 3 tablespoons of oil mixture.
3. Add brussels sprouts into the Air Fryer basket and cook at 370 °F (190 °C) for 20 minutes. Toss halfway through.
4. Now top with bacon and onion and cook for 10 minutes more.
5. Transfer brussels sprouts mixture into the large bowl. Add basil, avocado, and remaining oil mixture, and lemon juice and toss well.
6. Serve and enjoy.

 Cal: 248kcal | Carb: 13g | Fat: 16.5g | Prot: 11.7g | Saturated Fat 15.5g | Sugar 4.5g | Cholesterol 21mg

32. <u>Spinach Tomato Frittata</u>

 10 minutes   7 minutes

 17 mins  2

2 eggs
¼ cup fresh spinach, chopped
¼ cup tomatoes, chopped
2 tbsp. cream
1 tbsp. cheddar cheese, grated

Spray Air Fryer pan w/ cooking spray and set aside. In a bowl, whisk eggs with the remaining ingredients.
Pour egg mixture into the pan. Place pan in the Air Fryer basket and cook at 330 °F (170 °C) for 7 minutes.

 Cal: 90kcal | Carb: 1.8g | Fat: 6.3g | Prot: 16.8g | Sugar 1.2g | Cholesterol 170mg

AIR-FRYER MEAT: LAMB, BEEF, POULTRY, GAME, PORK

33. <u>Beef and Fruit Stir-Fry</u>

 15 minutes

 6 to 11 minutes

 21 mins

 2

- 12 oz. (340 g) sirloin tip steak, thinly sliced
- 1 tbsp. freshly squeezed lime juice
- 1 c. canned mandarin orange segments, drained, juice reserved (see Tip)
- 1 c. canned pineapple chunks, drained, juice reserved (see Tip)
- 1 teaspoon low-sodium soy sauce
- 1 tbsp. cornstarch
- 1 teaspoon olive oil
- 2 scallions, white and green parts, sliced
- Brown rice, cooked (optional)

1. In a medium bowl, mix the steak with the lime juice. Set aside.

2. In a small bowl, thoroughly mix 3 tablespoons of reserved mandarin orange juice, 3 tablespoons of reserved pineapple juice, the soy sauce, and cornstarch.

3. Drain the beef and transfer it to a medium metal bowl, reserving the juice. Stir the reserved juice into the mandarin-pineapple juice mixture. Set aside.

4. Add the olive oil and scallions to the steak. Place the metal bowl in the Air Fryer and cook for 3 to 4 minutes, or until the steak is almost cooked, shaking the basket once during cooking.

5. Stir in the mandarin oranges, pineapple, and juice -mixture. Cook for 3 to 7 minutes more, or until the sauce is bubbling and the beef is tender and reaches at least 145 °F (60 °C) on a meat thermometer.

6. Stir and serve over hot cooked brown rice, if desired.

Cal: 212kcal | Carb: 28g | Fat: 4g | Prot: 19g | Saturated Fat 1g | Sodium 105mg | Fiber 2g | Sugar 22g

34. Seasoned Beef Roast

 10 minutes   45 minutes

 55 mins   2

- 3 lb. beef top roast
- 1 tbsp. olive oil
- 2 tbsp. Montreal steak seasoning

1. Coat the roast with oil and then rub with the seasoning generously.
2. With kitchen twines, tie the roast to keep it compact.
3. Arrange the roast onto the cooking tray.
4. Arrange the drip pan in the bottom of the Air Fryer Oven cooking chamber.
5. Select "Air Fry" and then adjust the temperature to 360 °F (180 °C).
6. Set the timer for 45 minutes and press the "Start".
7. When the display shows "Add Food" insert the cooking tray in the center position.
8. When the display shows "Turn Food" do nothing.
9. When cooking time is complete, remove the tray & place the roast onto a platter for about 10 minutes before slicing.
10. W/ a sharp knife, cut the roast into desired-sized slices, and serve.

Cal: 269kcal | Fat: 9.9g | Saturated Fat 3.4g | Cholesterol 122mg | Sodium 538mg

35. Beef Burgers

 15 minutes   18 minutes

 33 mins   2

For Burgers:
- 1-lb. ground beef
- ½ c. panko breadcrumbs
- ¼ c. onion, chopped finely
- 3 tbsp. Dijon mustard
- 3 tsp. low-sodium soy sauce
- 2 tsp. fresh rosemary, chopped finely
- Salt, to taste

For Topping:
- 2 tbsp. Dijon mustard
- 1 tbsp. brown sugar

- 1 teaspoon soy sauce
- 4 Gruyere cheese slices

1. In a large bowl, add all the ingredients and mix until well combined.
2. Make 4 equal-sized patties from the mixture.
3. Arrange the patties onto a cooking tray.
4. Arrange the drip pan in the bottom of the Air Fryer Oven cooking chamber.
5. Select "Air Fry" and then adjust the temperature to 370 °F (190 °C).
6. Set the timer for 15 minutes and press the "Start".
7. When the display shows "Add Food" insert the cooking rack in the center position.
8. When the display shows "Turn Food" turn the burgers.
9. Meanwhile, for the sauce: In a small bowl, add the mustard, brown sugar, and soy sauce and mix well.
10. When cooking time is complete, remove the tray and coat the burgers with the sauce.
11. Top each burger with 1 cheese slice.
12. Return the tray to the cooking chamber and select "Broil".
13. Set the timer for 3 minutes and press the "Start".
14. When cooking time is complete, remove the tray and serve hot.

Cal: 402kcal | Fat: 18g | Saturated Fat 8.5g | Cholesterol 133mg | Sodium 651mg |
Total Carbs: 6.3 g | Fiber: 0.8 g | Sugar: 3 g |
Protein: 44.4 g

36. **Beef Jerky**

 15 minutes   3 hours

 3 h and 15 mins   2

- 1½ lb. beef round, trimmed
- ½ c. Worcestershire sauce
- ½ c. low-sodium soy sauce
- 2 tsp. honey
- 1 tsp. liquid smoke
- 2 tsp. onion powder
- ½ tsp. red pepper flakes
- Ground black pepper, as required

1. In a zip-top bag, place the beef and freeze for 1-2 hours to firm up.
2. Place the meat onto a cutting board and cut against the grain into ⅛-¼-inch strips.
3. In a large bowl, add the remaining ingredients and mix until well combined.
4. Add the steak slices and coat with the mixture generously.
5. Refrigerate to marinate for about 4-6 hours.
6. Remove the beef slices from the bowl and with paper towels, pat dry them.

7. Divide the steak strips onto the cooking trays and arrange them in an even layer.
8. Select "Dehydrate" and then adjust the temperature to 160 °F (70 °C) in your Air Fryer.
9. Set the timer for 3 hours and press the "Start".
10. When the display shows "Add Food" insert 1 tray in the top position and another in the center position.
11. After 1½ hours, switch the position of cooking trays.
12. Meanwhile, in a small pan, add the remaining ingredients over medium heat and cook for about 10 minutes, stirring occasionally.
13. When cooking time is complete, remove the trays.

 Cal: 372kcal | Carb: 12g | Fat: 10.7g | Prot: 53.8g | Saturated Fat 4g | Cholesterol 152mg | Sodium 2000mg | Fiber 0.2g | Sugar 11.3g

37. **Sweet & Spicy Meatballs**

 20 minutes   30 minutes

 50 mins   2

For Meatballs:
- 2 lb. lean ground beef
- 2/3 c. quick-cooking oats
- ½ c. Ritz crackers, crushed
- 1 (5-ounce) can evaporated milk
- 2 large eggs, beaten lightly
- 1 tsp. honey
- 1 tbsp. dried onion, minced
- 1 tsp. garlic powder
- 1 tsp. ground cumin
- Salt and ground black pepper, as required

For Sauce:
- 1/3 c. orange marmalade
- 1/3 c. honey
- 1/3 c. brown sugar
- 2 tbsp. cornstarch
- 2 tbsp. soy sauce
- 1-2 tbsp. hot sauce
- 1 tbsp. Worcestershire sauce

1. For meatballs: in a large bowl, add all the ingredients and mix until well combined.
2. Make 1½-inch balls from the mixture.
3. Arrange half of the meatballs onto a cooking tray in a single layer.
4. Arrange the drip pan in the bottom of the Air Fryer Oven cooking chamber.
5. Select "Air Fry" and then adjust the temperature to 380 °F (190 °C) .
6. Set the timer for 15 minutes and press the "Start".
7. When the display shows "Add Food" insert the cooking tray in the center position.
8. When the display shows "Turn Food" turn the meatballs.

9. When cooking time is complete, remove the tray.
10. Repeat with the remaining meatballs.
11. Meanwhile, for the sauce: In a small pan, add all the ingredients over medium heat and cook until thickened, stirring continuously.
12. Serve the meatballs with the topping of sauce.

 Cal: 411kcal │ Fat: 11.1g │ Saturated Fat 4.1g │ Cholesterol 153mg │ Sodium 448mg │ Total Carbs: 38.8 g │ Fiber: 1 g │ Sugar: 28.1 g │ Protein: 38.9 g

38. <u>**Peas and Ham Muffins**</u>

 23 minutes   21 minutes

 44 mins   12

- 200 g peas
- 200 g flour
- 3 eggs
- 10 g yeast
- 100 g cooked ham
- 100 ml milk
- 100 g grated pecorino cheese
- 100 ml seed oil
- Extra virgin olive oil (to taste)
- 1 sprig of parsley
- Salt and pepper to taste

1. Preheat the Air Fryer to 325 °F (160 °C) .
2. Cook the ground sausage until golden brown.
3. Divide peas, ham into each muffin c.
4. Mix egg whites, eggs, salt, and pepper.
5. Pour egg mixture into ramekins and cook in deep fryer for 20 minutes.
6. Serve and enjoy.

 Cal: 489kcal │ Carb: 12.6g │ Fat: 35.6g │ Prot: 22.8g │ Fiber 3.8g

39. <u>**Spiced Pork Shoulder**</u>

 15 minutes   55 minutes

 1 h and 10 mins   2

- 1 tsp. ground cumin
- 1 tsp. cayenne pepper

- 1 tsp. garlic powder
- Salt and ground black pepper, as required
- 2 lb. skin-on pork shoulder

1. In a small bowl, mix together the spices, salt, and black pepper.
2. Arrange the pork shoulder onto a cutting board, skin-side down.
3. Season the inner side of the pork shoulder with salt and black pepper.
4. With kitchen twines, tie the pork shoulder into a long round cylinder shape.
5. Season the outer side of pork shoulder with spice mixture.
6. Insert the rotisserie rod through the pork shoulder.
7. Insert the rotisserie forks, one on each side of the rod to secure the pork shoulder.
8. Arrange the drip pan in the bottom of the Air Fryer Oven cooking chamber.
9. Select "Roast" and then adjust the temperature to 350 °F (180 °C).
10. Set the timer for 55 minutes and press the "Start".
11. When the display shows "Add Food" press the red lever down and load the left side of the rod.
12. Now, slide the rod's left side into the groove along the metal bar so it doesn't move.
13. Then, close the door and touch "Rotate".
14. When cooking time is complete, press the red lever to release the rod.
15. Remove the pork and place it onto a platter for about 10 minutes before slicing.
16. With a sharp knife, cut the pork shoulder into desired-sized slices and serve.

Cal: 445kcal | Carb: 0.7g | Fat: 32.5g | Prot: 35.4g | Saturated Fat 11.9g | Cholesterol 136mg | Sodium 131mg | Fiber 0.2g | Sugar 0.2g

40. Crispy Mustard Pork Tenderloin

 10 minutes   12-16 minutes

 22 mins   2

- ½ tbsp. low-sodium grainy mustard
- ½ tsp. olive oil
- ¼ tsp. dry mustard powder
- 1 (1-lb.) pork tenderloin, silver skin, and excess fat trimmed and discarded (see Tip, here)
- 2 slices low-sodium whole-wheat bread, crumbled
- ¼ c. ground walnuts (see Tip)
- ½ tbsp. cornstarch

1. In a small bowl, stir together the mustard, olive oil, and mustard powder. Spread this mixture over the pork.
2. On a plate, mix the bread crumbs, walnuts, and cornstarch. Dip the mustard-coated pork into the crumb -mixture to coat.

3. Air-fry the pork for 12 to 16 minutes, or until it registers at least 145 °F (60 °C) on a meat thermometer. Slice to serve.

 Cal: 239kcal | Carb: 15g | Fat: 9g | Prot: 26g | Saturated Fat 2g | Sodium 118mg | m Fiber 2g | Sugar 3g

41. **Apple Pork Tenderloin**

 10 minutes   14-19 minutes

 24 mins   2

- 1 (1-lb.) pork tenderloin, cut into 4 pieces (see Tip)
- 1 tbsp. apple butter
- 2 teaspoons olive oil
- 2 Granny Smith apples or Jonagold apples, sliced
- 3 celery stalks, sliced
- 1 onion, sliced
- ½ teaspoon dried marjoram
- 1/3 c. apple juice

1. Rub each piece of pork with the apple butter and olive oil.
2. In a medium metal bowl, mix the pork, apples, celery, onion, marjoram, and apple juice.
3. Place the bowl into the Air Fryer and roast for 14 to 19 minutes, or until the pork reaches at least 145 °F (60 °C) on a meat thermometer and the apples and vegetables are tender. Stir once during cooking.
4. Serve immediately.

 Cal: 213kcal | Carb: 20g | Fat: 5g | Prot: 24g | Saturated Fat 1g | Sodium 88mg | Fiber 3g | Sugar 15g

42. **Espresso-Grilled Pork Tenderloin**

 15 minutes   9-11 minutes

 24 mins   2

- 1 tbsp. packed brown sugar
- 2 tsp. espresso powder
- 1 tsp. ground paprika
- ½ tsp. dried marjoram

- 1 tbsp. honey
- 1 tbsp. freshly squeezed lemon juice
- 2 tsp. olive oil
- 1 (1-lb.) pork tenderloin

1. In a small bowl, mix the brown sugar, espresso powder, paprika, and marjoram.
2. Stir in the honey, lemon juice, and olive oil until well mixed.
3. Spread the honey mixture over the pork and let stand for 10 minutes at room temperature.
4. Roast the tenderloin in the Air Fryer basket for 9 to 11 minutes, or until the pork registers at least 145 °F (60 °C) on a meat thermometer. Slice the meat to serve.

Cal: 177kcal | Carb: 10g | Fat: 5g | Prot: 23g | Saturated Fat 1g | Sodium 61mg | Fiber 1g | Sugar 8g

43. **Pork and Potatoes**

- 2 cups creamer potatoes, rinsed and dried
- 2 tsp. olive oil (see Tip)
- 1 (1-lb.) pork tenderloin, cut into 1-inch cubes
- 1 onion, chopped
- 1 red bell pepper, chopped
- 2 garlic cloves, minced
- ½ tsp. oregano, dried
- 2 tbsp. low-sodium chicken broth

1. In a medium bowl, toss the potatoes and olive oil to coat.
2. Transfer the potatoes to the Air Fryer basket. Roast for 15 minutes.
3. In a medium metal bowl, mix the potatoes, pork, onion, red bell pepper, garlic, and oregano.
4. Drizzle with the chicken broth. Put the bowl in the Air Fryer basket. Roast for about 10 minutes more, shaking the basket once during cooking, until the pork reaches at least 145 °F (60 °C) on a meat thermometer and the potatoes are tender. Serve immediately.

Cal: 235kcal | Carb: 22g | Fat: 5g | Prot: 26g | Saturated Fat 1g | Sodium 66mg | Fiber: 3 g | Sugar: 4 g

 5 minutes   25 minutes

 30 mins   2

44. **Pork and Fruit Kebabs**

 15 minutes   9-12 minutes

 24 mins   2

- 1/3c. apricot jam
- 2 tbsp. freshly squeezed lemon juice
- 2 tsp. olive oil
- ½ tsp. tarragon, dried
- 1 (1-lb.) pork tenderloin, cut into 1-inch cubes
- 4 plums, pitted and quartered (see Tip)
- 4 small apricots, pitted and halved (see Tip)

1. In a large bowl, mix the jam, lemon juice, olive oil, and tarragon.
2. Add the pork and stir to coat. Let stand for 10 minutes at room temperature.
3. Alternating the items, thread the pork, plums, and -apricots onto 4 metal skewers that fit into the Air Fryer. Brush with any remaining jam mixture. Discard any remaining marinade.
4. Grill the kebabs in the Air Fryer for 9 to 12 minutes, or until the pork reaches 145 °F (60

°C) on a meat thermometer and the fruit is tender.
5. Serve immediately.

 Cal: 256kcal | Carb: 30g | Fat: 5g | Prot: 24g | Saturated Fat 1g | Sodium 60mg | Fiber 2g | Sugar 22g

45. **Greek Vegetable Skillet**

 10 minutes   9 to 19 minutes

 19 mins   2

- ½ lb. 96% lean ground beef
- 2 medium tomatoes, chopped
- 1 onion, chopped
- 2 garlic cloves, minced
- 2 cups fresh baby spinach (see Tip)
- 2 tbsp. freshly squeezed lemon juice
- 1/3 c. low-sodium beef broth
- 2 tbsp. crumbled low-sodium feta cheese

1. In a 6-by-2-inch metal pan, crumble the beef. Cook in the Air Fryer for 3 to 7 minutes,

stirring once during cooking, until browned. Drain off any fat or liquid.

2. Add the tomatoes, onion, & garlic to the pan. Air-fry for 4 to 8 minutes more, or until the onion is tender.

3. Add the spinach, lemon juice, and beef broth. Air-fry for 2 to 4 minutes more, or until the spinach is wilted.

4. Sprinkle with the feta cheese and serve immediately

Cal: 97kcal | Carb: 5g | Fat: 1g | Prot: 15g | Saturated Fat 1g | Sodium 123mg | Fiber 1g | Sugar 2g

46.   **Hearty Crispy mustard pork tenderloin**

 10 minutes   15 minutes

 25 mins   4

- 3 tbsp. Low-Sodium grainy mustard
- 2 tbsp. olive oil
- ¼ tsp. dry mustard powder
- 1 (1-lb.) pork tenderloin, silver skin, and excess fat trimmed and discarded

- 2 slices low-sodium whole-wheat bread, crumbled
- ¼ c. ground walnuts
- 2 tbsp. cornstarch

- On a plate, mix the breadcrumbs, walnuts, and cornstarch. Dip the mustard-coated pork into the crumb mixture to coat.
- Preheat Air Fryer to 400 °F (200 °C) for 5 minutes. After 5 minutes, carefully place pork tenderloin into Air Fryer and air fry at 400 °F (200 °C) for 20-22 minutes. Internal temp should be 145 ° – 160 °F (70 °C) .
- When the Air Fryer cycle is complete, carefully remove pork tenderloin to a cutting board and let rest for 5 minutes before slicing.
- Slice to serve.

Cal: 300kcal | Carb: 13.6g | Fat: 11.9g | Prot: 33.6g | Sugar 1.7g | Cholesterol 81mg

47.   **Lamb Patties**

 10 minutes   20 minutes

 30 mins   **Serve: 4**

- 1 ½ lb. ground lamb
- 1/3 c. feta cheese, crumbled
- 1 tsp. oregano
- ¼ tsp. pepper
- ½ tsp. salt

1. Preheat the Air Fryer to 375 °F (190 °C) .
2. Add all ingredients into the bowl and mix until well combined.
3. Spray Air Fryer basket with cooking spray.
4. Make the equal shape of patties from the meat mixture and place them into the Air Fryer basket.
5. Cook lamb patties for 10 minutes then turn to another side and cook for 10 minutes more.
6. Serve and enjoy.

Cal: 351kcal | Carb: 0.8g | Fat: 15.2g | Prot: 49.6g | Sugar 0.5g | Cholesterol 164mg

48. **Lamb Meatballs**

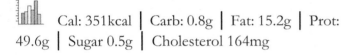

 10 minutes   14 minutes

 24 mins   **Serve:** 8

- 1 egg, lightly beaten
- 1 lb. ground lamb
- ¼ tsp. bay leaf, crushed
- 1 tsp. ground coriander
- ¼ tsp. cayenne pepper
- ¼ tsp. turmeric
- 1 onion, chopped
- 2 garlic cloves, minced
- ¼ tsp. pepper
- 1 tsp. salt

1. Preheat the Air Fryer to 400 °F (200 °C) .
2. Spray Air Fryer basket with cooking spray.
3. Add all ingredients into the large bowl & mix until well combined.
4. Make small balls from the meat mixture and place them into the Air Fryer basket and cook for 14 minutes. Shake basket twice while cooking.
5. Serve and enjoy.

Cal: 121kcal | Carb: 2g | Fat: 4g | Prot: 16g | Sugar 0.5g | Cholesterol 70mg

49. <u>Light Herbed Meatballs</u>

 10 minutes   12 to 17 minutes

 22 mins   2

- 1 medium onion, minced
- 2 garlic cloves, minced
- 1 tsp. olive oil
- 1 slice low-sodium whole-wheat bread, crumbled
- 3 tbsp. 1 percent milk
- 1 tsp. marjoram, dried
- 1 tsp. basil, dried
- 1-lb. 96 % lean ground beef

1. In a 6-by-2-inch pan, combine the onion, garlic, & olive oil. Air-fry for 2 to 4 minutes, or until the vegetables are crisp-tender.
2. Transfer the vegetables to a medium bowl, and add the bread crumbs, milk, marjoram, and basil. Mix well.
3. Add the ground beef. With your hands, work the mixture gently but thoroughly until combined. Form the meat mixture into about 24 (1-inch) meatballs.
4. Bake the meatballs, in batches, in the Air Fryer basket for 12 to 17 minutes, or until they reach 160 °F (70 °C) on a meat thermometer.
5. Serve immediately.

Cal: 190kcal | Carb: 8g | Fat: 6g | Prot: 25g | Saturated Fat 2g | Sodium 120mg | Fiber 1g | Sugar 2g | % DV 1mg | vitamin A 3mg | % DV vitamin Cmg

50. <u>Seasoned Pork Tenderloin</u>

 10 minutes   45 minutes

 55 mins   2

- 1½ lb. pork tenderloin
- 2-3 tbsp. BBQ pork seasoning

1. Rub the pork with seasoning generously.
2. Insert the rotisserie rod through the pork tenderloin.
3. Insert the rotisserie forks, one on each side of the rod to secure the pork tenderloin.

52

4. Arrange the drip pan in the bottom of the Air Fryer Oven cooking chamber.
5. Select "Roast" and then adjust the temperature to 360 °F (180 °C).
6. Set the timer for 45 minutes and press the "Start".
7. When the display shows "Add Food" press the red lever down and load the left side of the rod.
8. Now, slide the rod's left side into the groove along the metal bar so it doesn't move.
9. Then, close the door and touch "Rotate".
10. When cooking time is complete, press the red lever to release the rod.
11. Remove the pork and place it onto a platter for 10 minutes before slicing.
12. W/ a sharp knife, cut the roast into desired-sized slices & serve.

 Cal: 195kcal | Carb: 0g | Fat: 4.8g | Prot: 35.6g | Saturated Fat 1.6g | Cholesterol 99mg | Sodium 116mg | Fiber 0g | Sugar 0g

51. <u>**Glazed Pork Tenderloin**</u>

 15 minutes   20 minutes

 35 mins   2

- 1-lb. pork tenderloin
- 2 tbsp. Sriracha
- 2 tbsp. honey
- Salt, as required

1. Insert the rotisserie rod through a pork tenderloin.
2. Insert the rotisserie forks, one on each side of the rod to secure the pork tenderloin.
3. In a small bowl, add the Sriracha, honey, and salt and mix well.
4. Brush the pork tenderloin with the honey mixture evenly.
5. Arrange the drip pan in the bottom of the Air Fryer Oven cooking chamber.
6. Select "Air Fry" and then adjust the temperature to 350 °F (180 °C).
7. Set the timer for 20 minutes and press the "Start".
8. When the display shows "Add Food" press the red lever down and load the left side of the rod.
9. Now, slide the rod's left side into the groove along the metal bar so it doesn't move.
10. Then, close the door and touch "Rotate".
11. When cooking time is complete, press the red lever to release the rod.
12. Remove the pork and place it onto a platter for about 10 minutes before slicing.
13. W/ a sharp knife, cut the roast into desired-sized slices & serve.

Cal: 269kcal | Carb: 13.5g | Fat: 5.3g | Prot: 39.7g | Saturated Fat 1.8g | Cholesterol 110mg | Sodium 207mg | Fiber 0g | Sugar 11.6g

52. <u>Seasoned Pork Chops</u>

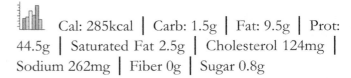 Cal: 285kcal | Carb: 1.5g | Fat: 9.5g | Prot: 44.5g | Saturated Fat 2.5g | Cholesterol 124mg | Sodium 262mg | Fiber 0g | Sugar 0.8g

 10 minutes 12 minutes

 22 mins 2

- 4 (6-lb.) boneless pork chops
- 2 tbsp. pork rub
- 1 tbsp. olive oil

1. Coat both sides of the pork chops with the oil and then, rub with the pork rub.
2. Place the pork chops onto the lightly greased cooking tray.
3. Arrange the drip pan in the bottom of the Air Fryer Oven cooking chamber.
4. Select "Air Fry" and then adjust the temperature to 400 °F (200 °C).
5. Set the timer for 12 minutes and press the "Start".
6. When the display shows "Add Food" insert the cooking tray in the center position.
7. When the display shows "Turn Food" turn the pork chops.
8. When cooking time is complete, remove the tray and serve hot.

53. <u>Cajun Bacon Pork Loin Fillet</u>

 10 minutes 20 minutes

 30 mins 2

- 1½ lb. pork loin fillet or pork tenderloin
- 3 tbsp. olive oil
- 2 tbsp. Cajun Spice Mix
- Salt
- 6 slices bacon
- Olive oil spray

1. Preparing the Ingredients. Cut the pork in half so that it will fit in the Air Fryer basket.
2. Place both pieces of meat in a resealable plastic bag. Add the oil, Cajun seasoning, and salt to taste, if using. Seal the bag & massage to coat all of the meat with the oil and

seasonings. Marinate in the refrigerator for at least 1 hr or up to 24 hours.

3. Air Frying. Remove the pork from the bag and wrap 3 bacon slices around each piece. Spray the Pro Breeze Air Fryer basket with olive oil spray. Place the meat in the Air Fryer. Set the Pro Breeze Air Fryer to 350 °F (180 °C) for 15 minutes. Increase the temperature to 400 °F (200 °C) for 5 minutes. Use a meat thermometer to ensure the meat has reached an internal temperature of 145 °F (60 °C) .

4. Let the meat rest for 10 minutes. Slice into 6 medallions and serve.

Cal: 355kcal | Carb: 0.6g | Fat: 22.9g | Prot: 34.8g

54. **Sweet & Spicy Country-Style Ribs**

 10 minutes 25 minutes

 35 mins 2

- 2 tbsp. brown sugar
- 2 tbsp. smoked paprika

- 1 tsp. garlic powder
- 1 tsp. onion powder
- 1 tsp. dry mustard
- 1 tsp. ground cumin
- 1 tsp. salt
- 1 tsp. black pepper
- ¼ to ½ teaspoon cayenne pepper
- 1½ lb. boneless country-style pork ribs
- 1 c. barbecue sauce

1. Preparing the Ingredients. In a small bowl, stir together the brown sugar, paprika, garlic powder, onion powder, dry mustard, cumin, salt, black pepper, and cayenne. Mix until well combined.

2. Pat the ribs dry with a paper towel. Generously sprinkle the rub evenly over both sides of the ribs and rub it with your fingers.

3. Air Frying. Place the ribs in the Air Fryer basket. Set the Pro Breeze Air Fryer to 350 °F (180 °C) for 15 minutes. Turn the ribs and brush with ½ c. of the barbecue sauce. Cook for an additional 10 minutes. Use a meat thermometer to ensure the pork has reached an internal temperature of 145 °F (60 °C) . Serve with remaining barbecue sauce.

Cal: 416kcal | Carb: 36.8g | Fat: 12.2g | Prot: 38.4g |

55. Honey-Mustard Chicken Breasts

 5 minutes   25 minutes

 30 mins   2

- 6 (6-oz, each) boneless, skinless chicken breasts
- 2 tbsp. fresh rosemary, minced
- 3 tbsp. honey
- 1 tbsp. Dijon mustard
- Salt and pepper to taste

1. Combine the mustard, honey, pepper, rosemary, and salt in a bowl. Rub the chicken with this mixture.

Grease the Air Fryer basket with oil. Air fry the chicken at 350 °F (180 °C) for 20 to 24 minutes or until the chicken reaches 165 °F (70 °C) . Serve.

Calories: 236 g | Carbs: 9.8 g | Fat 5 g | Protein: 38 g

56. Chicken Parmesan Wings

 5 minutes   15 minutes

 20 mins   2

- 2 lbs. chicken wings, cut into drumettes, pat dried
- ½ c. parmesan, plus 6 tbsp. grated
- 1 tsp. herbs de Provence
- 1 tsp. paprika
- Salt to taste

1. Combine the parmesan, herbs, paprika, and salt in a bowl and rub the chicken with this mixture. Preheat the Air Fryer at 350F.
2. Grease the basket with cooking spray. Cook for 15 minutes. Flip once at the halfway mark. Garnish with parmesan and serve.

 Cal: 490kcal | Carb: 1g | Fat: 22g | Prot: 72g

57. <u>Air Fryer Chicken</u>

 5 minutes   30 minutes

 35 mins   2

- 2 lbs. chicken wings
- Salt and pepper to taste
- Cooking spray

1. Flavor the chicken wings with salt and pepper. Grease the Air Fryer basket with cooking spray. Add chicken wings and cook at 400 °F (200 °C) for 35 minutes.
2. Flip 3 times during cooking for even cooking. Serve.

 Cal: 277kcal │ Carb: 1g │ Fat: 8g │ Prot: 50g

58. <u>Whole Chicken</u>

 5 minutes   40 minutes

 45 mins   2

- 1 (2 ½ pounds (1130 g)) Whole chicken, washed and pat dried
- 2 tbsp. dry rub
- 1 tsp. salt
- Cooking spray

1. Preheat the Air Fryer at 350F. Rub the dry rub on the chicken. Then, rub with salt. Cook it at 350 °F (180 °C) for 45 minutes. After 30 minutes, flip the chicken and finish cooking.

Chicken is done when it reaches 165 °F (70 °C) . Enjoy!

 Cal: 412kcal │ Carb: 1g │ Fat: 28g │ Prot: 35g

59. Honey Duck Breasts

 5 minutes   25 minutes

 30 mins   2

- 1 smoked duck breast, halved
- 1 tsp. honey
- 1 tsp. tomato paste
- 1 tbsp. mustard
- ½ tsp. apple vinegar

1. Mix tomato paste, honey, mustard, and vinegar in a bowl. Whisk well. Add duck breast pieces and coat well. Cook in the Air Fryer at 370 °F (190 °C) for 15 minutes.
2. Remove the duck breast from the Air Fryer and add to the honey mixture. Coat again. Cook again at 370F for 6 minutes. Serve.

 Cal: 274kcal | Carb: 22g | Fat: 11g | Prot: 13g |

60. Creamy Coconut Chicken

 5 minutes   20 minutes

 25 mins   2

- 4 big chicken legs
- 5 tsp. turmeric powder
- 2 tbsp. ginger, grated
- Salt and black pepper to taste
- 4 tbsp. coconut cream

1. In a bowl, mix salt, pepper, ginger, turmeric, and cream. Whisk.
2. Add chicken pieces, coat, and marinate for 2 hours.
3. Transfer chicken to the preheated Air Fryer and cook at 370 °F (190 °C) for 25 minutes.
4. Serve.

 Cal: 300kcal | Carb: 22g | Fat: 4g | Prot: 20g

61. Buffalo Chicken Tenders

 Cal: 160kcal | Carb: 0.6g | Fat: 4.4g | Prot: 27.3g

 5 minutes   20 minutes

 25 mins   2

- 1 lb. boneless, skinless chicken tenders
- ¼ c. hot sauce
- 1 1/2 oz. (14 g) pork rinds, finely ground
- 1 tsp. chili powder
- 1 tsp. garlic powder

1. Put the chicken breasts in a bowl and pour hot sauce over them. Toss to coat. Mix ground pork rinds, chili powder, and garlic powder in another bowl.
2. Place each tender in the ground pork rinds, and coat well. With wet hands, press down the pork rinds into the chicken. Place the tender in a single layer into the Air Fryer basket.
3. Cook at 375 °F (190 °C) for 20 minutes. Flip once.
4. Serve.

62. Teriyaki Wings

 5 minutes   20 minutes

 25 mins   2

- Chicken wings – 2 pound (910 g) s
- Teriyaki sauce – ½ c.
- Minced garlic – 2 tsp.
- Ground ginger - ¼ tsp.
- Baking powder – 2 tsp.

1. Except for the baking powder, place all ingredients in a bowl and marinate for 1 hour in the refrigerator. Place wings into the Air Fryer basket and sprinkle with baking powder.
2. Gently rub into wings. Cook at 400F for 25 minutes. Shake the basket two- or three-times during cooking. Serve.

Cal: 446kcal | Carb: 3.1g | Fat: 29.8g | Prot: 41.8g

63. <u>**Turkey Wraps with Sauce**</u>

 10 minutes   16 minutes

 26 mins   6

Wraps:

- 4 large collard leaves, stems removed
- 1 medium avocado, sliced
- ½ cucumber, thinly sliced
- 1 cup mango, diced
- 6 large strawberries, thinly sliced
- 6 (200 g) grilled turkey breasts, diced
- 24 mint leaves

Dipping Sauce:

- 2 tbsp. almond butter
- 2 tbsp. coconut cream
- 1 birds eye chili, finely chopped
- 2 tbsp. unsweetened applesauce
- ¼ cup fresh lime juice
- 1 tsp. sesame oil
- 1 tbsp. apple cider vinegar

- 1 tbsp. tahini
- 1 clove garlic, crushed
- 1 tbsp. grated fresh ginger
- ⅛ tsp. sea salt

For the chicken breasts:
1. Start by setting your Air Fryer toast oven to 350 °F (180 °C) .
2. Lightly coat the basket of the Air Fryer toast oven with oil.
3. Season the turkey with salt and pepper and arrange it on the basket and air fry for 8 minutes on each side.
4. Once done, remove from Air Fryer toast oven and set on a platter to cool slightly then dice them up.

For the wraps:
1. Divide the vegies and diced turkey breasts equally among the four large collard leaves; fold bottom edges over the filling, and then both sides and roll very tightly up to the end of the leaves; secure with toothpicks and cut each in half.

Make the sauce:
2. Combine all the sauce ingredients in a blender and blend until very smooth.
3. Divide between bowls and serve with the wraps.

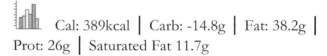 Cal: 389kcal | Carb: -14.8g | Fat: 38.2g | Prot: 26g | Saturated Fat 11.7g

64. <u>Air Roasted Chicken Drumsticks</u>

 10 minutes   20 minutes

 30 mins   4

- 1 tbsp. olive oil
- 1-½ red onions, diced
- 1-½ teaspoons salt
- 8 chicken drumsticks
- ½ teaspoon pepper
- ¼ teaspoon chili powder
- 2 tablespoons thyme leaves
- Zest of ¼ lemon
- 8 cloves of garlic
- 2/3 cup diced tinned tomatoes
- 2 tbsp. sweet balsamic vinegar

1. Set your Air Fryer toast oven to 370 °F (190 °C) and add the oil, onions, and ½ teaspoon of salt to the pan of your Air Fryer toast oven. Cook for 2 minutes until golden.
2. Add the chicken drumsticks & sprinkle w/ the rest of the salt, pepper, and chili, then add the thyme, garlic cloves, and lemon zest; add in balsamic vinegar and tomatoes and spread the mixture between the drumsticks.
3. Air roast for about 20 minutes or until done to desire.
4. Serve the creamy chicken over rice, pasta, or potatoes or with a side of vegetables.
5. Enjoy!

Cal: 329kcal | Carb: 60.5g | Fat: 0.4g | Prot: 20.8g | Saturated Fat 13.3g

65. <u>Air Roasted Whole Chicken</u>

 15 minutes   50 minutes

 1 h and 5 mins   12

- 1 full chicken, dissected
- 2 tablespoons extra virgin olive oil
- 2 tablespoons chopped garlic
- 2 teaspoons sea salt
- 1 teaspoon pepper
- 1 tablespoon chopped fresh thyme

- 1 tablespoon chopped fresh rosemary

Fruit Compote:

- 1 apple, diced
- ½ cup red grapes, halved, seeds removed
- 12 dried apricots, sliced
- 16 dried figs, coarsely chopped
- ½ cup red onion, chopped
- ½ cup cider vinegar
- ½ cup dry white wine
- 2 tsp. liquid stevia
- ½ teas tsp. poon salt
- ½ tsp. pepper

1. In a small bowl, stir together thyme, rosemary, garlic, salt, and pepper and rub the mixture over the pork.
2. Light your Air Fryer toast oven and set it to 320 °F (160 °C) , place the chicken on the basket, and air roast for 10 minutes.
3. Increase the temperature and cook for another 10 minutes, turning the chicken pieces once. Increase the temperature one more Time to 400 °F (200 °C) and cook for 5 minutes to get a crispy finish.
4. Make Fruit Compote: In a saucepan, combine all ingredients and cook over medium heat, stirring, for about 25 minutes or until liquid is reduced to a quarter.
5. Once the chicken is cooked, serve hot with a ladle of fruit compote Enjoy!

 Cal: 511kcal | Carb: 13.5g | Fat: 36.8g | Prot: 31.5g | Saturated Fat 15g

66. Italian Beef Roast

 10 minutes   45 minutes

 55 mins   6

- 2 ½ lbs. beef roast
- 2 tbsp. Italian seasoning
- 1 tsp. olive oil

1. Rub beef roast with oil and season with Italian seasoning, pepper, and salt.
2. Place the beef roast into the Air Fryer basket and cook at 350 °F (180 °C) for 45 minutes.
3. Slice and serve.

Cal: 372kcal | Carb: 0.5g | Fat: 13.9g | Prot: 57.4g | Sugar 0.4g | Cholesterol 172mg

67. Italian Meatballs

 10 minutes   11 minutes

 21 mins   4

- 1 egg
- 1 lb. ground beef
- 1 tsp. Italian seasoning
- 1 tbsp. onion, minced
- ¼ cup marinara sauce, sugar-free
- 1/3 cup parmesan cheese, shredded
- 1 tsp. garlic, minced

1. Spray Air Fryer basket with cooking spray.
2. Add ingredients into the mixing bowl and mix until well combined.
3. Make meatballs from mixture and place into the Air Fryer basket and cook at 350 °F (180 °C) for 12 minutes.
4. Enjoy!

Cal: 274kcal | Carb: 3.2g | Fat: 10.8g | Prot: 38.9g | Sugar 1.7g | Cholesterol 150mg

68. Burgers Patties

 10 minutes   10 minutes

 20 mins   2

- ½ lb. ground beef
- ¼ tsp. onion powder
- ¼ tsp. garlic powder
- 2 drops liquid smoke
- ½ tsp. hot sauce
- ½ tsp. dried parsley
- ¼ tsp. black pepper
- ½ tbsp. Worcestershire sauce
- ¼ tsp. salt

1. Spray Air Fryer basket with cooking spray.
2. Add the ingredients into the large mixing bowl and mix until combined.
3. Make patties from the mixture and place into the Air Fryer basket and cook at 350 °F (180 °C) for 10 minutes.
4. Turn patties halfway through.

Cal: 218kcal | Carb: 1.5g | Fat: 7.1g | Prot: 34.5g | Sugar 1g | Cholesterol 101mg

69. Tasty Beef Patties

 10 minutes   10 minutes

 20 mins   2

- ½ lb. ground beef
- 1 tsp. ginger, minced
- ½ tbsp. soy sauce
- 1 tbsp. gochujang
- ¼ tsp. salt
- 1 tbsp. green onion, chopped
- ½ tbsp. sesame oil

1. In a large bowl, mix together ground beef and the remaining ingredients. Place mixture in the refrigerator for 1 hour.

Make patties from the beef mixture and place them into the Air Fryer basket and cook at 360 °F (180 °C) for 10 minutes.

 Cal: 257kcal | Carb: 3.3g | Fat: 10.5g | Prot: 35g | Sugar 1.5g | Cholesterol 101mg

70. Flavorful Pork Chops

 10 minutes   16 minutes

 26 mins   4

- 4 pork chops, boneless
- 2 tsp. olive oil
- ½ tsp. celery seed
- ½ tsp. parsley
- ½ tsp. onion powder
- ½ tsp. garlic powder
- ½ tsp. salt

1. Brush pork chops with olive oil.
2. Mix together celery seed, parsley, onion powder, garlic powder, and salt and sprinkle over pork chops.
3. Place pork chops into the Air Fryer basket and cook at 350 °F (180 °C) for 16 minutes.
4. Turn pork chops halfway through.

Cal: 279kcal | Carb: 0.6g | Fat: 22.3g | Prot: 18.1g | Sugar 0.2g | Cholesterol 69mg

71. BBQ Pork Chops

 10 minutes   14 minutes

 24 mins   2

- 2 pork chops
- ½ tsp. sesame oil
- ¼ cup BBQ sauce, sugar-free
- 2 garlic cloves, minced

1. Spray Air Fryer basket with cooking spray.
2. Preheat the cosori Air Fryer to 350 F.
3. Add all ingredients into the mixing bowl and mix well and place in the fridge for 1 hour.
4. Place marinated pork chops into the Air Fryer basket and cook for 14 minutes. Turn halfway through.
5. Serve and enjoy.

Cal: 317kcal | Carb: 12.4g | Fat: 21.1g |
Prot: 18.2g | Sugar 8.2g | Cholesterol 69mg

72. Pesto Pork Chops

 10 minutes   18 minutes

 28 mins   5

- 5 pork chops
- 1 tbsp. basil pesto
- 2 tbsp. almond flour
- Pepper
- Salt

1. Spray pork chops with cooking spray.
2. Rub basil pesto on top of pork chops and coat with almond flour.
3. Place pork chops into the Air Fryer basket and cook at 350 °F (180 °C) for 18 minutes.
4. Serve and enjoy.

Cal: 320kcal | Carb: 2.4g | Fat: 25.5g |
Prot: 20.4g | Sugar 0.4g | Cholesterol 69mg

73. <u>Tender & Juicy Kebab</u>

 10 minutes 10 minutes

 20 mins 2

- ½ lb. ground beef
- 1 tbsp. parsley, chopped
- ½ tbsp. olive oil
- 1 tbsp. kabab spice mix
- ½ tbsp. garlic, minced
- ½ tsp. salt

1. Add all ingredients into the stand mixer until well combined.
2. Equally, divide the meat mixture into two portions and make two sausage shapes.

Place kababs into the Air Fryer basket and cook at 370 °F (190 °C) for 10 minutes.

Cal: 259kcal | Carb: 2.7g | Fat: 11.1g | Prot: 35.2g | Sugar 1.1g | Cholesterol 101mg

74. <u>Meatballs Surprise</u>

 10 minutes 20 minutes

 30 mins 2

- ½ lb. ground beef
- 2 tbsp. onion, chopped
- 1 ½ tbsp. mushrooms, diced
- 1 tbsp. parsley, chopped
- ¼ cup almond flour
- ¼ tsp. pepper
- ½ tsp. salt

1. In a mixing bowl, combine together all ingredients until well combined.
2. Make meatballs from the mixture and place them into the Air Fryer basket and cook at 350 F for 20 minutes.

Cal: 237kcal | Carb: 2.1g | Fat: 8.9g | Prot: 35.5g | Sugar 0.6g | Cholesterol 101mg

75. <u>Asian Beef</u>

 10 minutes   20 minutes

 30 mins   4

- 1 lb. flank steak, sliced
- 1 tsp. xanthan gum
- For sauce:
- 1 tsp. ground ginger
- 1 tbsp. chili sauce
- 1 garlic clove, crushed
- 2 tbsp. white wine vinegar
- 1 tbsp. water
- 1 tbsp. arrowroot powder
- ½ tsp. sesame seeds
- 1 tsp. liquid stevia
- ½ cup soy sauce

1. Toss sliced meat with xanthan gum.
2. Spray Air Fryer basket with cooking spray.
3. Add the meat into the Air Fryer basket and cook at 390 °F (200 °C) for 20 minutes. Turn meat halfway through.

4. Meanwhile, add remaining ingredients into the saucepan and heat over low heat until begins to boil.
5. Add cooked meat to the sauce and coat well.
6. Serve and enjoy.

Cal: 253kcal │ Carb: 6.2g │ Fat: 9.7g │ Prot: 33.8g │ Sugar 0.7g │ Cholesterol 62mg

76. <u>Tasty Ginger Garlic Beef</u>

 10 minutes   20 minutes

 30 mins   4

- 1 lb. beef tips, sliced
- 1 tbsp. ginger, sliced
- 2 tbsp. garlic, minced
- 2 tbsp. sesame oil
- 1 tbsp. fish sauce
- 2 tbsp. coconut aminos
- 1 tsp. xanthan gum
- ¼ cup scallion, chopped
- 2 red chili peppers, sliced
- 2 tbsp. water

1. Spray Air Fryer basket with cooking spray.
2. Toss beef with xanthan gum together.
3. Add beef into the Air Fryer basket and cook at 390F for 20 minutes. Turn halfway through.
4. Meanwhile, in a saucepan, add remaining ingredients except for green onion and heat over low heat. Once it begins boiling, then remove it from heat.
5. Add cooked meat into the saucepan and stir to coat. Let sit in the saucepan for 5 minutes.
6. Transfer in serving dish and top with green onion and serve.

Cal: 349kcal | Carb: 5.7g | Fat: 21.9g | Prot: 31.4g | Sugar 0.5g | Cholesterol 93mg

77. <u>Beef Fillet with Garlic Mayo</u>

 10 minutes   40 minutes

 50 mins   8

- 3 lb. beef fillet
- 1 cup mayonnaise
- 4 tbsp. Dijon mustard
- 1/3 cup sour cream
- ¼ cup tarragon, chopped
- 2 tbsp. chives, chopped
- 2 cloves garlic (minced)
- Salt and black pepper, to taste

1. Preheat the Air Fryer to 370 °F (190 °C) .
2. Season beef using salt and pepper, transfer to the Air Fryer and cook for 20 minutes. Remove and set aside.
3. In a bowl, whisk the mustard and tarragon. Add the beef and toss, return to the Air Fryer and cook for 20 minutes.
4. In a separate bowl, mix the garlic, sour cream, mayonnaise, chives, salt, and pepper. Whisk and set aside.
5. Serve the beef with the garlic-mayo spread.

 Cal: 400kcal | Carb: 26g | Fat: 12g | Prot: 19g |

FISH AND SEAFOOD

78. Breaded Coconut Shrimp

4. Dip the cleaned shrimp into the flour, egg wash, and finish it off with the coconut mixture.
5. Lightly spray the basket of the fryer and set the timer for 10-15 minutes.
6. Air-fry until it's golden brown before serving.

 Cal: 285kcal | Carb: 3.7g | Fat: 12.8g | Prot: 38.1g

79. Breaded Cod Sticks

 5 minutes   15 minutes

 20 mins   4

- 450 g shrimp
- 1 c. panko breadcrumbs
- 1 c. shredded coconut
- 2 eggs
- 1/3 c. all-purpose flour

1. Fix the temperature of the Air Fryer at 360 °F (180 °C) .
2. Peel and devein the shrimp.
3. Whisk the seasonings with the flour as desired. In another dish, whisk the eggs, and in the third container, combine the breadcrumbs and coconut.

 5 minutes   20 minutes

 25 mins   4

- 2 large eggs
- 3 tbsp. milk
- 2 cups breadcrumbs
- 1 c. almond flour
- 450 g Cod

1. Heat the Air Fryer at 350 °F (180 °C) .
2. Prepare three bowls; one with the milk and eggs, one with the breadcrumbs (salt and pepper if desired), and another with almond flour.
3. Dip the sticks in the flour, egg mixture, and breadcrumbs.
4. Place in the basket and set the timer for 12 minutes.
5. Toss the basket halfway through the cooking process.
6. Serve with your favorite sauce.

 Cal: 254kcal | Carb: 5.7g | Fat: 14.2g | Prot: 39.1g

80. **Codfish Nuggets**

 5 minutes   20 minutes

 25 mins   4

- 450 g Cod fillet
- 3 eggs
- 4 tbsp. olive oil

- 1 c. almond flour
- 1 c. gluten-free breadcrumbs

1. Heat the Air Fryer to 390 °F (200 °C) .
2. Slice the cod into nuggets.
3. Prepare three bowls. Whisk the eggs in one. Combine the salt, oil, and breadcrumbs in another. Sift the almond flour into the third one.
4. Cover each of the nuggets with the flour, dip in the eggs, and the breadcrumbs.
5. Arrange the nuggets in the basket and set the timer for 20 minutes.
6. Serve the fish with your favorite dips or sides.

 Cal: 334kcal | Carb: 8g | Fat: 10g | Prot: 32g

81. **Creamy Salmon**

 5 minutes   20 minutes

 25 mins   4

- 1 tbsp. chopped dill
- 1 tbsp. olive oil

- 3 tbsp. sour cream
- 1.76 oz. (50 g) plain yogurt
- 340 g salmon

1. Heat the Air Fryer and wait for it to reach 285 °F (140 °C) .
2. Shake the salt over the salmon and add them to the fryer basket with the olive oil to air-fry for 10 minutes.
3. Whisk the yogurt, salt, and dill.
4. Serve the salmon with the sauce with your favorite sides.

 Cal: 340kcal | Carb: 5g | Fat: 16g | Prot: 32g

82. Crumbled Fish

 5 minutes   15 minutes

 20 mins   4

- ½ c. breadcrumbs
- 4 tbsp. vegetable oil
- 1 egg
- 4 fish fillets

- 1 lemon

1. Heat the Air Fryer to reach 356 °F (180 °C) .
2. Whisk the oil and breadcrumbs until crumbly.
3. Dip the fish into the egg, then the crumb mixture.
4. Arrange the fish in the cooker and air-fry for 12 minutes.
5. Garnish using the lemon.

 Cal: 320kcal | Carb: 8g | Fat: 10g | Prot: 28g

83. Fried Catfish

 5 minutes   15 minutes

 20 mins   4

- 1 tbsp. olive oil
- ¼ c. seasoned fish fry
- 4 Catfish fillets

1. Heat the Air Fryer to reach 400 °F (200 °C) before fry time.
2. Rinse the catfish and pat dry using a paper towel.
3. Dump the seasoning into a sizeable zipper-type bag. Add the fish and shake to cover each fillet. Spray with a spritz of cooking oil spray and add to the basket.
4. Set the timer for 10 minutes. Flip, and reset the timer for ten additional minutes. Turn the fish once more and cook for 2-3 minutes.
5. Once it reaches the desired crispiness, transfer to a plate, and serve.

 Cal: 376kcal | Carb: 10g | Fat: 9g | Prot: 28g

84. <u>Zucchini with Tuna</u>

 10 minutes   30 minutes

 40 mins   4

- 4 medium zucchinis
- 120 g of tuna in oil (canned) drained
- 30 g grated cheese
- 1 c. pine nuts

- Salt, pepper to taste

1. Cut the zucchini in half laterally and empty it with a small spoon (set aside the pulp that will be used for filling); place them in the basket.
2. In a food processor, put the zucchini pulp, drained tuna, pine nuts, and grated cheese. Mix everything until you get a homogeneous and dense mixture.
3. Fill the zucchini. Set the Air Fryer to 360 °F (180 °C) .
4. Simmer for 20 min. depending on the size of the zucchini. Let cool before serving

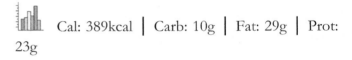 Cal: 389kcal | Carb: 10g | Fat: 29g | Prot: 23g

85. <u>Caramelized Salmon Fillet</u>

 5 minutes   25 minutes

 30 mins   4

- 2 salmon fillets
- 60 g cane sugar

- 4 tbsp. soy sauce
- 50 g sesame seeds
- Fresh Ginger

1. Preheat the Air Fryer at 360 °F (180 °C) for 5 minutes.
2. Put the sugar and soy sauce in the basket.
3. Cook everything for 5 minutes.
4. In the meantime, wash the fish well, pass it through sesame to cover it completely and place it inside the tank and add the fresh ginger.
5. Cook for 12 minutes.
6. Turn the fish over and finish cooking for another 8 minutes.

Cal: 569kcal | Carb: 40g | Fat: 14.9g | Prot: 66.9g

86. <u>**Deep-Fried Prawns**</u>

 15 minutes   20 minutes

 35 mins   6

- 12 prawns

- 2 eggs
- Flour to taste
- Breadcrumbs
- 1 tsp. oil

1. Remove the head of the prawns and shell carefully.
2. Pass the prawns first in the flour, then in the beaten egg, and then in the breadcrumbs.
3. Preheat the Air Fryer for 1 minute at 30 °F (150 °C) .
4. Add the prawns and cook for 4 minutes. If the prawns are large, it will be necessary to cook 6 at a time.
5. Turn the prawns and cook for another 4 minutes.
6. They should be served with a yogurt or mayonnaise sauce.

Cal: 2385kcal | Carb: 52.3g | Fat: 23g | Prot: 21.4g

87. <u>**Monkfish with Olives and Capers**</u>

 25 minutes   40 minutes

1 h and 5 mins   4

- 1 monkfish
- 10 cherry tomatoes
- 50 g cailletier olives
- 5 capers

1. Spread aluminum foil inside the Air Fryer basket and place the monkfish clean and skinless.
2. Add chopped tomatoes, olives, capers, oil, and salt.
3. Set the temperature to 320 °F (160 °C) .
4. Cook the monkfish for about 40 minutes.

 Cal: 404kcal | Carb: 36g | Fat: 29g | Prot: 24g

88. **Shrimp, Zucchini and Cherry Tomato Sauce**

 5 minutes   30 minutes

 35 mins   4

- 2 zucchinis
- 300 g shrimp
- 7 cherry tomatoes
- Salt and pepper to taste
- 1 garlic clove

1. Pour the oil into the Air Fryer, add the garlic clove, and diced zucchini.
2. Cook for 15 minutes at 60 °F (150 °C) .
3. Add the shrimp and the pieces of tomato, salt, and spices.
4. Cook for another 5 to 10 minutes or until the shrimp water evaporates.

 Cal: 214kcal | Carb: 7.8g | Fat: 8.6g | Prot: 27g

89. **Salmon with Pistachio Bark**

 10 minutes   30 minutes

 40 mins   4

- 600 g salmon fillet
- 50 g pistachios
- Salt to taste

1. Put the parchment paper on the bottom of the Air Fryer basket and place the salmon fillet in it (it can be cooked whole or already divided into four portions).
2. Cut the pistachios into thick pieces; grease the top of the fish, salt (little because the pistachios are already salted), and cover everything with the pistachios.
3. Set the Air Fryer to 360 °F (180 °C) and simmer for 25 minutes.

Cal: 372kcal | Carb: 9.4g | Fat: 21.8g | Prot: 34.7g

90. **Tasty Chipotle Shrimp**

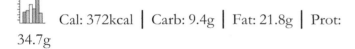

 10 minutes   8 minutes

 18 mins   4

- 1 ½ lb. shrimp, peeled & deveined
- 2 tbsp. olive oil

- 4 tbsp. lime juice
- 1 /4 tsp. ground cumin
- 2 tsp. chipotle in adobo

1. Add shrimp, oil, lime juice, cumin, and chipotle in a zip-lock bag. Seal bag, shake well, and place it in the refrigerator for 30 minutes.
2. Thread marinated shrimp onto skewers and place skewers into the Air Fryer basket.
3. Cook at 350 °F (180 °C) for 8 minutes.

 Cal: 274kcal | Carb: 6.4g | Fat: 10g | Prot: 39g | Sugar 0.7g | Cholesterol 359mg

91. **Tasty Shrimp Fajitas**

 10 minutes   22 minutes

 32 mins   12

- 1 lb. shrimp, tail-off
- 2 tbsp. taco seasoning
- ½ cup onion, diced
- 1 green bell pepper, diced
- 1 red bell pepper, diced

1. Spray Air Fryer basket with cooking spray.
2. Add shrimp, taco seasoning, onion, and bell peppers into the mixing bowl and toss well.
3. Place shrimp mixture into the Air Fryer basket and cook at 390 °F for 12 minutes.
4. Stir shrimp mixture and cook for 10 minutes more.

Cal: 55kcal | Carb: 2.7g | Fat: 0.8g | Prot: 9g | Sugar 1.2g | Cholesterol 80mg

SNACK & BREAD, WRAPS, AND SANDWICHES, PIZZA

92. Fresh Pizza

 10-20 minutes   30-45 minutes

 40 mins   1

- 70 ml of water
- 125 g flour
- 3 g salt
- 7 g fresh yeast
- 100 g of tomato
- 100 g mozzarella
- Oregano to taste

1. Pour the flour into a bowl, form a well, and then add the other ingredients in the center. Knead with your hands until you get a soft and flexible dough. Form a ball with this dough, and then let it grow in a priorly floured bowl.
2. Cover wi/ a clean cloth and let stand at room temperature, away from drafts. After about 1 hour of lifting, starts spreading the dough preheat the Air Fryer to 300 °F (150 °C) for 5 minutes.
3. Grease the bottom and spread the pizza dough. Cover with tomato coulis. Add a pinch of salt and oregano. After 15 minutes of cooking, add the diced mozzarella. Approximately after 10 minutes, turn the pizza half a turn.
4. Cook for an additional 7 minutes.

 Cal: 290kcal | Carb: 36g | Fat: 11g | Prot: 11g

93. Frozen Pizza

 5 minutes   15-30 minutes

 20 mins   1

- 1 piece Frozen Pizza

1. Cook in the Air fryer for 20 minutes at 70 °F (180 °C) , turning after 15 minutes.
2. Enjoy!

 Cal: 576kcal | Carb: 62g | Fat: 26g | Prot: 22g |

94. Crispy Baked Avocado Tacos

 10 minutes   20 minutes

 30 mins   5

Salsa:

- 1 c. finely chopped pineapple
- 1 Roma tomato, finely chopped
- ½ red bell pepper, finely chopped
- ½ of a medium red onion
- 1 garlic clove minced
- ½ jalapeno finely chopped
- Pinch each cumin and salt

Avocado tacos:

1. 1 avocado
2. ¼ c. all-purpose flour (35 g)
3. 1 large egg whisked
4. ½ c. panko crumbs (65 g)
5. Pinch each salt and pepper
6. 4 flour tortillas

Adobo Sauce:

- ¼ c. plain yogurt (60 g)
- 2 tbsp. Mayonnaise (30 g)
- ¼ tsp. lime juice

- 1 tbsp. Adobo sauce from a jar of chipotle peppers

Polte peppers

1. Salsa: Combine all the salsa ingredients and put them in the fridge.
2. Prepare avocado: Halve the length of the avocado and remove the pit. Lay the avocado skin face down and cut each half into 4 equal pieces. Then gently peel off the skin.
3. Preparation station: Preheat the oven to 450 °F (230 °C) or the Air Fryer to 370 °F (190 °C) . Arrange your work area so that you have a bowl of flour, a bowl of whisk, a bowl of Panko with S&P, and a baking sheet lined with parchment at the end.
4. Coat: Dip each avocado slice first in the flour, then in the egg, and then in the panko. Place on the prepared baking sheet and bake for 10 minutes or fry in the air. Lightly brown after half of the cooking process.
5. Sauce: While cooking avocados, combine all the sauce ingredients.
6. Serve: Put salsa on a tortilla, top with 2 pieces of avocado, and drizzle with sauce. Serve immediately and enjoy!

 Cal: 193kcal | Carb: 4.7g | Fat: 13.3g | Prot: 13.7g

95. Mozzarella Sticks with Marinara Sauce

 15 minutes   1 hour + 10 minutes

 1 h and 25 mins   12 cheese bites or 6 servings

- 1 egg, lightly beaten
- 1 tbsp. water
- ½ c. all-purpose flour
- ½ tbsp. salt
- ½ tsp. dried Italian seasoning
- ¾ c. panko breadcrumbs
- 6 Mozzarella cheese sticks
- Cooking spray
- ¾ c. marinara sauce

1. Slice the cheese sticks in half—crosswise.
2. Whisk egg with water in a shallow mixing dish.
3. Stir the flour with salt and Italian seasoning in another shallow dish.
4. Place breadcrumbs in a third shallow dish.
5. Dip the cheese sticks into the egg mixture, then cover using the flour mixture. Dredge again into the egg mix, then into breadcrumbs until coated.
6. Arrange them on a baking tray—freeze until firm (1 hr.).
7. Preheat the Air Fryer to reach 360 °F (180 °C).
8. Lightly coat the fryer basket using a spritz of cooking spray.
9. Place frozen cheese bites in the Air Fryer (single-layered), working in batches if necessary, being careful not to crowd.
10. Cook in the preheated Air Fryer until golden brown and cheese just begins to melt (4-6 min.). Repeat with the rest of the bites.
11. Meanwhile, whisk the marinara sauce and red pepper to your liking.
12. Serve the bites with marinara sauce.

Cal: 183kcal | Carb: 22.6g | Fat: 5.4g | Prot: 10.9g | Fat Content 6.7g

96. Lighten-Up Air-Fried Empanadas

 10 minutes   30 minutes

40 mins 2

- 1 tbsp. olive oil
- 85 g 85/15 lean ground beef
- ¼ c. white onion
- 85 g cremini mushrooms
- 2 tsp. garlic
- 6 pitted green olives
- ¼ tsp. paprika
- ¼ tsp. ground cumin
- ⅛ tsp. ground cinnamon
- ½ c. tomatoes
- 8 square gyoza wrappers
- 1 Eg, lightly beaten

1. Heat the Air Fryer unit to reach 400 °F (200 °C).
2. Finely chop the onion, mushrooms, olives, and garlic. Also, chop the tomatoes or use canned.
3. Heat the oil in a skillet using the med-high temperature setting.
4. Add beef and onion to cook, stirring to crumble until brown (3 min.).
5. Mix in the mushrooms, occasionally stirring, until the mushrooms start to brown (6 min.).
6. Toss in the garlic, olives, paprika, cumin, and cinnamon; cook until mushrooms are very tender and have released most of their liquid (3 min.).
7. Stir in tomatoes and cook for one minute, stirring intermittently.
8. Transfer the filling to a holding container and wait for it to cool (5 min.).
9. Arrange four wrappers on the work surface. Place about 1½ tablespoons of filling in the middle of each wrapper. Brush each of the wrap's edges with egg and fold the wrappers over while pinching its edges to seal.
10. Repeat the process w/ the rest of the wrappers and filling.
11. Place four empanadas in the fryer basket (single-layered), and air-fry them until nicely browned (7 min.).
12. Repeat with the remaining empanadas.

 Cal: 343kcal | Carb: 25g | Fat: 19.4g | Prot: 17g | Fat Content 19g

97. **Cheesy Beef Sandwiches**

 5 minutes 30 minutes

 35 mins 8

- 2 garlic cloves, minced
- 2 onions, julienned
- ½ c. pickled pepper rings
- 1 package Italian salad dressing mix
- 4 slices provolone cheese
- 3-lb. beef top sirloin steak, sliced
- 2 large red peppers, julienned
- ½ tsp. beef base

- ½ tsp. pepper
- 1 can condensed French onion soup, undiluted

1. In a pressure cooker, combine the first 7 ingredients. Set the pressure and cook on high for 10 minutes. Put in the peppers and pepper rings. Pressure cook on high for 5 minutes.
2. Add beef, cheese, and vegetables to the bun bottoms. Air fryer for 1-2 minutes and serve.

 Cal: 4852kcal | Carb: 360g | Fat: 67g | Prot: 86g

98. Zucchini Chips

 10 minutes   15 minutes

 25 mins   5

- lb. zucchini
- ½ c. all-purpose flour
- 1 tsp. smoked paprika or your favorite seasoning
- 1 tsp. Italian seasoning

- ¼ c. Parmesan/similar cheese, finely shredded
- Black pepper & salt, as desired
- 2 eggs
- 2 cups breadcrumbs
- Cooking oil spray, as required

1. Heat the Air Fryer unit to 400 °F (200 °C).
2. Spritz the fryer basket with a tiny bit of cooking oil spray.
3. Break the eggs and add the flour and breadcrumbs into individual bowls.
4. Slice the zucchini into chips (¼-inch thick). Use a mandolin for precise slicing to make the chips close to the same size for even cooking.
5. Whisk the flour with salt, pepper, and paprika with a little shredded cheese.
6. Dip the zucchini pieces in the flour, egg, and lastly, the breadcrumbs before placing them in the fryer basket.
7. Spray the zucchini chips with cooking oil spray and air-fry for five minutes.
8. Open the basket and flip the chips to spritz them with a tiny bit more oil.
9. Air-fry the zucchini chips until nicely browned (4-7 min.) to serve.

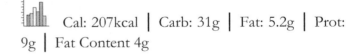 Cal: 207kcal | Carb: 31g | Fat: 5.2g | Prot: 9g | Fat Content 4g

99. Air-Fried Avocado Fries

 10 minutes   7-10 minutes

 17 mins   2

- 2 tbsp. all-purpose flour
- ⅛ tsp. salt
- ¼ tsp. black pepper
- ½ egg
- ½ tsp. water
- ½ ripe avocado
- ¼ c. panko breadcrumbs
- Cooking spray

1. Preheat the Air Fryer unit to 400 °F (200 °C).
2. Mix flour, pepper, and salt together in a shallow mixing container.
3. Whisk the egg and water in a second shallow container. Put the panko in a third shallow bowl.
4. Slice the avocado in half. Discard the seeds and peel.
5. Slice the prepared avocado into eight pieces.
6. Dredge an avocado slice through the flour, shaking off excess.

7. Immerse it into the egg and allow excess to drop off. Finally, press the slice into the panko, so both sides are covered.
8. Set on a plate and repeat with the remaining slices.
9. Generously spritz the avocado slices using a cooking oil spray.
10. Arrange the slices in the bowl of the Air Fryer, sprayed-side down. Spray the top side of the avocado slices as well.
11. Cook in the preheated Air Fryer for four minutes.
12. Turn avocado slices over and cook until golden (3 min.).

 Cal: 319kcal | Carb: 39.8g | Fat: 13.7g | Prot: 9.3g | Fat Content 18g

100. Chicken Pepper Nachos

 10 minutes   7 minutes

 17 mins   6

- 1 tbsp. bean stew powder
- 1 tsp. ground cumin
- 1 tsp. salt

- ½tsp. ground dark pepper
- 1 tsp. garlic powder
- ½tsp. new cleaved cilantro
- 1 pound (450 g) ground chicken
- 1-pound (450 g) red chime peppers cut into strips
- 1 ½cups ground cheddar

1. Preheat your Air Fryer to 400 °F (200 °C) .
2. Combine the flavors in a little bowl.
3. Add the turkey to an enormous skillet and cook until caramelized. Mix in the zest blend.
4. Spot the ringer pepper strips in a softly lubed heating container and top with the cooked chicken and cheddar.
5. Spot the skillet noticeable all-around fryer and cook for 8 minutes to soften and gently earthy colored the cheddar. Serve hot!

 Cal: 362kcal | Carb: 8g | Fat: 22g | Prot: 7g

101. **Cranberry Dark Chocolate Granola Bars**

 10 minutes   25 minutes

 35 mins   8

- 1 c. unsweetened shredded coconut
- 1 c. cut almonds
- ½ c. cleaved walnuts
- 1/3 c. dried cranberries
- 1/3 c. unsweetened, dim chocolate chips
- ½ c. hemp seeds
- ½ tsp. salt
- ½ c. margarine
- 2 tsp. keto maple syrup
- ½ c. powdered erythritol
- ½ tsp. vanilla

1. Preheat your Air Fryer to 300 °F (150 °C) and line the Air Fryer plate with material paper.
2. Add the coconut, nuts, and hemp seeds to a food processor and pulse until very much blended and brittle.
3. Spot the blend in an enormous bowl alongside the cranberries, dull chocolate chips, and salt.
4. In a little pot, dissolve the spread and maple syrup over low warmth.
5. Rush in the erythritol and mix until softened. Mood killer the warmth and add the vanilla concentrate.
6. Pour the margarine blend over the nut blend and mix rapidly to cover uniformly.
7. Pour the blend onto the readied sheet plate and press down, so the blend is leveled and even. Attempt to reduce it however much as could reasonably be expected, so the bars hold together well.
8. Spot the plate on the stove and heat for 20 minutes. The edges should turn marginally brown.
9. Cool the bars totally and afterward, cut and serve!

Cal: 179kcal | Carb: 6g | Fat: 16g | Prot: 3g

102. **Bacon Muffin Bites**

 20 minutes　　 25 minutes

 45 mins　　 24 little biscuits

- 6 tbsp. liquefied spread
- ¼ c. minced garlic
- ½ c. acrid cream
- 4 eggs
- 2 cups almond flour
- 1 c. coconut flour
- 2 tsp. preparing powder
- 1 c. destroyed cheddar
- ¼ c. cleaved parsley
- ½ c. cooked, chopped bacon

1. Preheat your Air Fryer to 325 °F (160 °C) and shower little biscuit tin or individual small-scale biscuit cups with cooking spray.
2. Spot the harsh cream, 1 tbsp. garlic, eggs, and salt in a food processor, and puree until smooth.

3. Add the flours, cheddar, and parsley to the food processor and heartbeat until a smooth mixture structure.
4. Overlap in the bacon disintegrates.
5. Scoop the player into the biscuit cups.
6. Join the liquefied margarine and the leftover garlic and afterward, brush the highest points of every biscuit with the spread blend.
7. Spot the biscuits noticeable all-around fryer and heat for 18 minutes or until the tops are brilliant earthy colored.
8. Cool before serving and appreciate!

 Cal: 198kcal | Carb: 5g | Fat: 1g | Prot: 12g

103. **Lemon Pepper Broccoli Crunch**

 5 minutes　　 6 Hours

 6 h and 5 mins　　 4

- 4 cups broccoli florets, slashed into reduced down pieces
- 1 tbsp. olive oil
- 1 tsp. ocean salt
- 1 tsp. lemon pepper preparing

1. Preheat your Air Fryer to 135 °F (60 °C) .
2. Wash and channel the broccoli florets.
3. Spot the broccoli in an enormous bowl and throw it with the olive oil and ocean salt.
4. Add the broccoli to the container of your Air Fryer or spread them in a level layer on the plate of your Air Fryer (either choice will work!).
5. Cook in the Air Fryer for around 6 hours, throwing the broccoli consistently to cook equitably. Basically, you will get dried out the broccoli.
6. When the broccoli is completely dried, take it out from the Air Fryer, throw with the lemon pepper preparing, and then, let cool. It will continue to be fresh as it cools.
7. Appreciate new or store in a hermetically sealed compartment for as long as a month.

 Cal: 53kcal | Carb: 1g | Fat: 3g | Prot: 2g

104. **<u>Delicate Garlic Parmesan Pretzels</u>**

 15 minutes   14 minutes

 29 mins   6

- 2 cups almond flour
- 1 tbsp. preparing powder
- 1 tsp. garlic powder
- 1 tsp. onion powder
- 3 eggs
- 5 tbsp. mollified cream cheddar
- 3 cups mozzarella cheddar, ground
- 1 tsp. ocean salt
- ½ tsp. garlic powder
- ¼ c. parmesan cheddar

1. Preheat your Air Fryer to 400 °F (200 °C) and set up the Air Fryer plate with material paper.
2. Spot the almond flour, onion powder, preparing powder, and 1 tsp. garlic powder in a big bowl and mix well.
3. Join the cream cheddar and mozzarella in a different bowl and dissolve in the microwave, warming gradually and mixing a few times to guarantee the cheddar liquefies and doesn't consume.
4. Add two eggs to the almond flour blend alongside the dissolved cheddar. Mix well until a mixture forms.
5. Separate the batter into six equivalent pieces and fold it into your ideal pretzel shape.
6. Spot the pretzels on the readied sheet plate.
7. Whisk the excess eggs and brush over the pretzels; at that point, sprinkle them all with the ocean salt, parmesan, and ½ tsp. garlic powder.
8. Heat in the Air Fryer for 12 minutes or until the pretzels are brilliant earthy colored.
9. Eliminate from the Air Fryer and appreciate while warm!

 Cal: 493kcal | Carb: 10g | Fat: 39g | Prot: 28g

105. Cucumber Chips

 15 minutes   3 Hours

 3 h and 15 mins   4

- 4 cups dainty cucumber cuts
- 2 tbsp. apple juice vinegar
- 2 tsp. ocean salt

1. Preheat your Air Fryer to 200 °F (90 °C) .
2. Spot the cucumber cuts on a paper towel and layer another paper towel on top to ingest the dampness in the cucumbers.
3. Spot the dried cuts in a huge bowl and throw them with the vinegar and salt.
4. Spot the cucumber cuts on a plate fixed with material and afterward, prepare a noticeable all-around fryer for 3 hours. The cucumbers will start to twist and brown somewhat.
5. Turn off the Air Fryer and let the cucumber cuts cool inside the fryer (this will help them dry somewhat more).
6. Appreciate immediately or store in an impermeable holder.

 Cal: 15kcal │ Carb: 4g │ Fat: 0g │ Prot: 1g

106. Cajun Cauliflower Crunch

 5 minutes   6 Hours

 6 h and 5 mins   4

- 4 cups cauliflower florets, chopped into scaled-down pieces
- 1 tbsp. olive oil
- 1 tsp. ocean salt
- 1 tsp. Cajun preparing

1. Preheat your Air Fryer to 135 °F (60 °C) .
2. Wash and channel the cauliflower florets.
3. Spot the cauliflower in a huge bowl and throw it with the olive oil and ocean salt.
4. Add the cauliflower to the crate of your Air Fryer or spread them in a level layer on the plate of your Air Fryer (either alternative will work!).
5. Cook noticeable all-around fryer for around 6 hours, throwing the cauliflower consistently to cook uniformly. Basically, you will dry out the cauliflower.
6. When the cauliflower is completely dried, eliminate it from the Air Fryer, throw with

the Cajun preparing, and then, let cool. It will continue to be fresh as it cools.

7. Appreciate new or store in a water/airproof holder for as long as a month.

 Cal: 59kcal | Carb: 4g | Fat: 3g | Prot: 1g

107. Sprouts Wraps

 5 minutes   20 minutes

 25 mins   12

- 12 bacon strips
- 12 Brussels sprouts a drizzle of olive oil

1. Wrap each Brussels sprouts in a bacon strip, brush them with some oil, put them in your Air Fryer's basket, and cook at 350 °F (180 °C) for 20 minutes.
2. Serve as a snack.

 Cal: 140kcal | Carb: 4g | Fat: 5g | Prot: 4g

108. Chocolate Donuts

 5 minutes   20 minutes

 25 mins   8-10

- (8-oz. (230 g)) can jumbo biscuits
- cooking oil
- chocolate sauce, such as Hershey's

1. Separate the biscuit dough into 8 biscuits and place them on a flat work surface. Use a small circle cookie cutter or a biscuit cutter to cut a hole in each biscuit center. You can also cut the holes using a knife.
2. Grease the basket with cooking oil.
3. Place 4 donuts in the Air Fryer oven. Do not stack. Spray with cooking oil. Cook for 4 minutes.
4. Open the Air Fryer & flip the donuts. Cook for an additional 4 minutes.
5. Remove the cooked donuts from the Air Fryer Oven, then repeat for the remaining 4 donuts.
6. Drizzle chocolate sauce over the donuts and enjoy while warm.

 Cal: 181kcal | Carb: 42g | Fat: 98g | Prot: 3g

109. **Coconut Pancake**

 10 minutes   20 minutes

 30 mins   4

- 2 cups self-rising flour
- 2 tbsp. sugar
- 2 eggs
- 1 and ½ cups coconut milk
- A drizzle of olive oil

1. In a bowl, mix eggs with sugar, milk, flour, and whisk until you obtain a batter.
2. Grease your Air Fryer with the oil, add the batter, spread into the pot, cover, and cook on Low for 20 minutes.
3. Slice pancake, divide between plates, and serve cold.

 Cal: 162kcal | Carb: 7g | Fat: 3g | Prot: 8g

SAUCES, DIPS, AND DRESSINGS, FRENCH FRIES

SAUCES, DIPS, AND DRESSINGS, FRENCH FRIES

110. Jalapeno Cheese Dip

 Cal: 227kcal | Carb: 25.3g | Fat: 10g | Prot: 9g | Saturated Fat 27g

111. Chicken and Parsley Sauce

 10 minutes   16 minutes

 26 mins   6

- ½ c. Monterey jack cheese, shredded
- ½ c. cheddar cheese, shredded
- Jalapeno pepper, minced
- 1tsp. garlic powder
- 1/3 c. sour cream
- 1/3 c. mayonnaise
- ½ oz. (14 g) cream cheese, softened
- ½ bacon slices, cooked and crumbled
- Pepper Salt

1. Preheat the Air Fryer to 325 °F (160 °C) .
2. Add all ingredients into the bowl and mix until combined.
3. Transfer bowl mixture into the Air Fryer baking dish and place in the Air Fryer and cook for 16 minutes.
4. Serve and enjoy.

 30 min   25 min

 55 mins   6

- 1 c. parsley, chopped
- 1 teaspoon oregano, dried
- ½ c. olive oil
- ¼ c. red wine
- 4 garlic cloves
- A pinch of salt
- A drizzle of maple syrup
- 12 chicken thighs

1. In your food processor, mix parsley with oregano, garlic, salt, oil, wine, and maple syrup and pulse really well.
2. In a bowl, mix chicken with parsley sauce, toss well, and keep in the fridge for 30 minutes.
3. Drain chicken, transfer to your Air Fryer's basket, and cook at 380 °F (190 °C) for 25 minutes, flipping the chicken once.
4. Divide chicken on plates, drizzle parsley sauce all over, and serve.

Cal: 354kcal | Carb: 22g | Fat: 10g | Prot: 17g | Fiber 12g

112. **<u>Duck Breast with Fig Sauce</u>**

 10 min   20 min

 30 mins   4

- 2 duck breasts, skin on, halved
- 1 tbsp. olive oil
- ½ tsp. thyme, chopped
- ½ tsp. garlic powder
- ¼ tsp. sweet paprika
- Salt and black pepper to the taste
- 1 c. beef stock
- 3 tbsp. butter, melted
- 1 shallot, chopped
- ½ c. port wine
- 4 tbsp. fig preserves
- 1 tbsp. white flour

1. Season duck breasts with salt and pepper, drizzle half of the melted butter, rub well, put in your Air Fryer's basket, and cook at 350 °F (180 °C) for 5 minutes on each side.
2. Meanwhile, heat up a pan with the olive oil and the rest of the butter over medium-high heat, add shallot, stir and cook for 2 minutes.
3. Add thyme, garlic powder, paprika, stock, salt, pepper, wine, and figs, stir and cook for 7-8 minutes.
4. Add flour, stir well, cook until sauce thickens a bit and take off the heat.
5. Divide duck breasts on plates, drizzle figs sauce all over, and serve.

Cal: 246kcal | Carb: 22g | Fat: 12g | Prot: 3g | Fiber 4g

113. <u>Parmesan French Fries</u>

 Cal: 445kcal | Carb: 25g | Fat: 27g | Prot: 20g | Fiber 2g

 15 minutes   15 minutes

 30 mins   6

- 1 lb. French fries
- ½ c. mayonnaise
- 2 cloves garlic, minced
- 1 tbsp. oil
- Salt and pepper to taste
- 1 tsp. garlic powder
- ½ c. Parmesan cheese, grated
- 1 tsp. lemon juice

1. Add a crisper basket to your Air Fryer.
2. Select the air fry function.
3. Set it to 375 °F (190 °C) for 22 minutes.
4. Press start to preheat.
5. Add fries to the basket.
6. Cook for 10 minutes.
7. Shake and cook for another 5 minutes.
8. Toss in oil and sprinkle with Parmesan cheese.
9. Mix the remaining ingredients in a bowl.
10. Serve fries with this sauce.

114. <u>Chicken Tenders and Flavored Sauce</u>

 10 min   10 minutes

 20 mins   6

- 1 teaspoon chili powder
- 2 teaspoon garlic powder
- 1 teaspoon onion powder
- 1 teaspoon sweet paprika
- Salt and black pepper to the taste
- 2 tablespoons butter
- 2 tablespoons olive oil
- 2 pound (910 g) s chicken tenders
- 2 tablespoons cornstarch
- ½ c. chicken stock
- 2 cups heavy cream
- 2 tablespoons water
- 2 tablespoons parsley, chopped

1. In a bowl, mix garlic powder with onion powder, chili, salt, pepper, and paprika, stir, add chicken and toss.
2. Rub chicken tenders with oil, place in your Air Fryer & cook at 360 °F (180 °C) for 10 minutes.
3. Meanwhile, heat up a pan w/ the butter over medium-high heat, add cornstarch, stock, cream, water, and parsley, stir, cover, and cook for 10 minutes.
4. Divide chicken on plates, drizzle sauce all over, and serve.

 Cal: 351kcal | Carb: 20g | Fat: 12g | Prot: 17g | Fiber 9g

115. Kale Dip

 10 minutes   12 minutes

 22 mins   6

- 1 lb kale, wash and chopped
- 1 cup heavy cream
- 1 onion, diced
- 1 tsp. butter
- 1/2 oz. (14 g) parmesan cheese, shredded

- ¼ tsp. pepper
- 1 tsp. salt

1. Add all ingredients into the Air Fryer baking dish and stir well.
2. Preheat the Air Fryer to 250 °F (120 °C) .
3. Place dish in the Air Fryer and cook for 12 minutes.
4. Serve and enjoy.

 Cal: 117kcal | Carb: -8.8g | Fat: 12g | Prot: 11g | Saturated Fat 27g

116. Chicken and Apricot Sauce

 10 min   20 min

 30 mins   4

- 1 whole chicken, cut into medium pieces
- Salt and black pepper to the taste
- 1 tbsp. olive oil
- ½ tsp. smoked paprika
- ¼ c. white wine

- ½ tsp. marjoram, dried
- ¼ c. chicken stock
- 2 tbsp. white vinegar
- ¼ c. apricot preserves
- 1 and ½ teaspoon ginger, grated
- 2 tbsp. honey

1. Season chicken with salt, pepper, marjoram, and paprika, toss to coat, add oil, rub well, place in your Air Fryer & cook at 360 °F (180 °C) for 10 minutes.
2. Transfer chicken to a pan that fits your Air Fryer, add stock, wine, vinegar, ginger, apricot preserves, and honey, toss, put in your Air Fryer, and cook at 360 °F (180 °C) for 10 minutes more.
3. Divide chicken and apricot sauce among plates and serve.

Cal: 200kcal | Carb: 20g | Fat: 7g | Prot: 14g | Fiber 19g

117. **Chicken and Green Onions Sauce**

 10 minutes   16 minutes

 TOT 26 mins   4

- 10 green onions, roughly chopped
- 1 inch piece ginger root, chopped
- 4 garlic cloves, minced
- 2 tbsp. fish sauce
- 3 tbsp. soy sauce
- 1 tsp. Chinese five-spice
- 10 chicken drumsticks
- 1 c. coconut milk
- Salt and black pepper to the taste
- 1 tsp. butter, melted
- ¼ c. cilantro, chopped
- 1 tbsp. lime juice

1. In your food processor, mix green onions with ginger, garlic, soy sauce, fish sauce, five-spice, salt, pepper, butter, and coconut milk and pulse well.
2. In a bowl, mix chicken with green onions mix, toss well, transfer everything to a pan that fits your Air Fryer & cook at 370 °F (190 °C) for 16 minutes, shaking the fryer once.
3. Divide among plates, sprinkle cilantro on top, drizzle lime juice and serve with a side salad.

Cal: 321kcal | Carb: 22g | Fat: 12g | Prot: 20g | Fiber 12g

118. Easy Carrot Dip

 10 minutes   15 minutes

 25 mins   6

- 2 cups carrots, grated
- ¼ tsp. cayenne pepper
- ½ tbsp. butter, melted
- 1tbsp. chives, chopped
- Pepper Salt

1. Add Ingredients into a Air Fryer baking dish and stir until well combined.
2. Place dish in the Air Fryer and cook at 380 °F (190 °C) for 15 minutes.
3. Transfer cook carrot mixture into the blender and blend until smooth.
4. Serve and enjoy.

Cal: 211kcal | Carb: 7.2g | Fat: 9g | Prot: 9g | Sugar 3.4g | Cholesterol 155mg

119. Roasted Garlic Dip

 10 minutes   20 minutes

 30 mins   6

- 2 head garlic
- ½ tbsp. olive oil

1. Slice the top off the garlic.
2. Drizzle with olive oil.
3. Add to the Air Fryer.
4. Set it to roast.
5. Cook at 390 °F (200 °C) for 20 minutes.
6. Peel the garlic.
7. Transfer to a food processor.
8. Pulse until smooth.

 Cal: 207kcal | Carb: 15.8g | Fat: 12g | Prot: 9g | Saturated Fat 17g

120. <u>Chicken Wings and Mint Sauce</u>

 20 min   16 min

 36 mins   6

- 18 chicken wings, halved
- 1 tbsp. turmeric powder
- 1 tbsp. cumin, ground
- 1 tbsp. ginger, grated
- 1 tbsp. coriander, ground
- 1 tbsp. sweet paprika
- Salt and black pepper to the taste
- 2 tbsp. olive oil

For the Mint Sauce:

- Juice from ½ lime
- 1 c. mint leaves
- 1 small ginger piece, chopped
- ¾ c. cilantro
- 1 tbsp. olive oil
- 1 tbsp. water
- Salt and black pepper to the taste
- 1 Serrano pepper, chopped

1. In a bowl, mix 1 tablespoon ginger with cumin, coriander, paprika, turmeric, salt, pepper, cayenne, and 2 tablespoons oil and stir well.
2. Add chicken wings pieces to this mix, toss to coat well, and keep in the fridge for 10 minutes.
3. Transfer chicken to your Air Fryer's basket and cook at 370 °F (190 °C) for 16 minutes, flipping them halfway.
4. In your blender, mix mint with cilantro, 1 small ginger piece, juice from ½ lime, 1 tablespoon olive oil, salt, pepper, water, and Serrano pepper, and blend very well.
5. Divide chicken wings on plates, drizzle the mint sauce all over, and serve.

 Cal: 300kcal | Carb: 27g | Fat: 15g | Prot: 16g | Fiber 11g

DESSERTS

DESSERTS

121. Simple Poached Pears

 5 minutes   10 minutes

 15 mins   6

- 6 firm pears, peeled
- 4 garlic cloves, minced
- 1 stick cinnamon
- 1 fresh ginger, minced
- 1 bottle of dry red wine
- 1 bay leaf
- Mixed Italian herbs as needed
- 1 and 1/3 cups stevia

1. Peel the pears leaving the stems attached.
2. Pour wine into your Air Fryer.
3. Add cinnamon, cloves, and ginger, bay leaf, and stevia, stir gently.
4. Add pears to the pot.
5. Close the lid.
6. Cook for 9 minutes on HIGH.
7. Quickly release the pressure.

8. Take the pears out using a tong, keep them on the side.
9. Set Sauté mode, make the mixture in half.
10. Drizzle the mixture with pears.
11. Serve and enjoy!

Cal: 150kcal | Carb: 2g | Fat: 16g | Prot: 0.5g | Saturated Fat 4g | Fiber 0g | Sodium 13mg

122. Cheesy Cauliflower Steak

 10 minutes   30 minutes

 40 mins   4

- 1 tbsp. mustard
- 1 head cauliflower
- 1 tsp. avocado mayonnaise
- ½ c. parmesan cheese, grated
- ¼ c. butter, cut into small pieces

1. Set your Air Fryer to Sauté mode and add butter and cauliflower.
2. Sauté for 3 minutes.
3. Add remaining ingredients and stir.
4. Lock lid and then cook on HIGH pressure for about 25-30 minutes.
5. Release pressure naturally over 10 minutes.
6. Serve and enjoy!

Cal: 155kcal | Carb: 4g | Fat: 13g | Prot: 6g | Saturated Fat 2g | Fiber 2g | Sodium 162mg

123. **Garlic and Mushroom Munchies**

 10 minutes 8 minutes

 18 mins 4

- ¼ c. vegetable stock
- 2 tbsp. extra virgin olive oil
- 1 tbsp. Dijon mustard
- 1 tsp. thyme, dried
- 1 tsp. of sea salt
- ½ tsp. rosemary, dried
- ¼ tsp. fresh ground black pepper

- 2 lb. cremini mushrooms, cleaned
- 6 garlic cloves, minced
- ¼ c. fresh parsley, chopped

1. Take a small bowl and whisk in vegetable stock, mustard, olive oil, salt, thyme, pepper, and rosemary.
2. Add mushrooms, garlic, and stock mix to your Air Fryer.
3. Close lid and cook on SLOW COOK Mode (LOW) for 8 hours.
4. Open the lid and stir in parsley.
5. Serve and enjoy!

Cal: 92kcal | Carb: 8g | Fat: 5g | Prot: 4g | Saturated Fat 2g | Fiber 2g | Sodium 550mg

124. **Lemon Mousse**

 10 minutes 12 minutes

 22 mins 2

- 1-2 ounces cream cheese, soft
- ½ teaspoon lemon liquid stevia
- ½ c. heavy cream

- ⅛ c. fresh lemon juice
- 2 pinch salt

1. In a bowl, add heavy cream, cream cheese, stevia, lemon juice, and salt
2. Pour the mixture into a ramekin and transfer to Air Fryer
3. Close the lid
4. Set Bake/Roast mode
5. Bake for 12 minutes to 350 °F (180 °C)
6. Check the doneness it before removing from the Air Fryer
7. Serve and enjoy!

Cal: 292kcal | Carb: 8g | Fat: 26g | Prot: 5g | Saturated Fat 8g | Fiber 1g | Sodium 30mg

125. **Pumpkin Carrot Pudding**

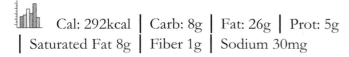

 10 minutes   20 minutes

 30 mins   2

- 2 cups pumpkin, pureed
- 2 cups carrots, shredded
- 2 whole eggs

- 1 tsp. granulated Erythritol
- 1 tsp. ground nutmeg
- 1 tbsp. extra-virgin olive oil
- ½ sweet onion, finely chopped
- 1 c. heavy whip cream
- ½ c. cream cheese, soft
- ¼ c. pumpkin seeds, garnish
- ¼ c. water
- ½ tsp. salt

1. Add oil to your Air Fryer and whisk in pumpkin, carrots, heavy cream, cream cheese, eggs, erythritol, onion, nutmeg, water, and salt.
2. Stir gently and close the lid.
3. Cook for 10 minutes on HIGH.
4. Release pressure naturally over 10 minutes.
5. Top with the pumpkin seeds.
6. Serve and enjoy!

Cal: 239kcal | Carb: 7g | Fat: 19g | Prot: 6g | Saturated Fat 4g | Fiber 2g | Sodium 423mg

126. <u>Spiced Baked Apple and Homemade Apple Spice</u>

 5 minutes   10 minutes

 15 mins   4

- 4 smalls to medium-sized apples
- 2 tbsp. coconut oil
- 2 tbsp. sugar
- 2 tbsp. ground cinnamon
- 2 tsp. ground nutmeg
- 1 ½ tsp. allspice

1. In a medium bowl, mix cinnamon, nutmeg, and allspice.
2. Pour into a small air-tight container.
3. Shake well to make sure the spice is well mixed.
4. Wash, peel, and slice the apples into rounds. Place them in a bowl.
5. Melt the coconut oil in a small saucepan on the stove.
6. Drizzle melted coconut oil over the sliced apples.
7. Sprinkle the apples with homemade apple spice and sugar.
8. Use a spoon to stir the apples to make sure the spice and coconut oil covers all the apple slices.
9. Use non-stick cooking spray to spray the cake pan.
10. Preheat the Air Fryer to 350 °F (180 °C). Use the Air Fry setting and set the Preheat for 3 minutes.
11. Place the apple slices in the cake pan.
12. Place the cake pans in the preheated Air Fryer.
13. Set the Air Fryer for 10 minutes and use the Air Fry setting to start baking the apple slices.
14. At 5 minutes, pause the Air Fryer, open the Air Fryer draw to check, and turn the apple slices.
15. Start the Air Fryer to cook the apples for the last 5 minutes.
16. After 10 minutes, the Air Fryer will switch off. The apples should be cooked through.
17. Once the apples are cooked, remove the Air Fryer drawer and place it on the cooling rack or mat.
18. Remove the cake pan from the Air Fryer, use oven gloves.
19. Divide into portions and serve.

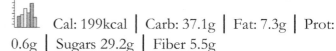 Cal: 199kcal | Carb: 37.1g | Fat: 7.3g | Prot: 0.6g | Sugars 29.2g | Fiber 5.5g

127. <u>Sugar Dough Dippers</u>

 17 minutes   8 minutes

 25 mins   4

- 1 tsp. white sugar
- 2 cups all-purpose flour
- ¼ tsp. baking soda
- ½ tsp. baking powder
- 1 flat teaspoon salt
- 4 tbsp. butter
- ½ c. buttermilk
- 2 tbsp. whole fresh milk

1. In a bowl, sieve together 1 ½ cups of flour, salt, baking soda, and baking powder.
2. Put 1 tablespoon of the butter aside.
3. Use the leftover butter to rub into the flour mix to make a crumbling mixture.
4. Pour the buttermilk into the mixture, stir with a cake spatula until the mixture turns into dough. Do not over mix, you want it to be a nice manageable dough texture.
5. Clean a working surface and sprinkle some flour over it. This is where you are going to cut out the biscuits from the dough.
6. Manipulate the dough into a round shape that is at least ½ inch thick.
7. Use a round cookie-cutter that is not too large, cut out 10 round dough shapes.
8. Use non-stick cooking spray to spray the Air Fryer drawer.
9. Line the Air Fryer drawer with Air Fryer parchment paper.
10. Preheat the Air Fryer to 400 °F (200 °C) . Use the Air Fry setting and set the Preheat for 3 minutes.
11. Melt the last block of butter in a small saucepan on the stovetop.
12. Brush the cookies with melted butter.
13. Place the cookies in the Air Fryer. Do not crowd and only use one layer to fill the Air Fryer drawer.
14. Set fryer for 8 minutes and use the Air Fry setting to start cooking the dessert.

15. After 8 minutes, the Air Fryer will switch off. The dough balls should be golden brown and cooked through.
16. Once the dough dippers are cooked, remove the Air Fryer drawer and place it on the cooling rack or mat.
17. Remove the dough dippers by using the spatula or food tongs.
18. Divide into portions and serve.

Cal: 469kcal | Carb: 77.7g | Fat: 12.8g | Prot: 10.6g | Sugars 12.1g | Fiber 2.4g

128. <u>**Churro Donuts**</u>

 35 minutes   55 minutes

 1 h and 30 mins   12

- ¼ tsp. salt
- ¼ c. plus 2 tbsp. unsalted butter, divided
- ½ c. all-purpose flour
- 1/3 c. white sugar
- 2 tsp. cinnamon
- 4 oz. (110 g) baking chocolate (bittersweet is the best)

- 2 large fresh eggs (do not use eggs from the fridge)
- 2 tbsp. heavy cream
- ½ c. fresh water
- 2 tbsp. vanilla yogurt

1. On the stovetop at medium heat, bring the water to a boil in a saucepan.
2. When the water is boiling, add ¼ c. butter and salt.
3. Add flour and take the heat down one notch on the stove.
4. Use a wooden spoon or whisk, mix the flour and water mix into a dough.
5. The mixture will start to smooth out in about 30 seconds.
6. Stir the mixture until the dough starts to get a bit stiff. It will start to come away from the sides of the saucepan. This process takes about 3 minutes, you will know when it is ready because it forms a film at the bottom of the pan.
7. Pour the mixture into a heatproof, clean bowl when it is ready.
8. Keep stirring the mixture for about 1 to 2 minutes, or until the mixture has cooled down a bit.
9. If the mixture is no longer piping hot, add the eggs and stir vigorously.
10. After mixing, pour into a piping bag.
11. The mixture needs to be set in the refrigerator for at least 30 minutes.
12. Spray the bottom of the Air Fryer drawer with non-stick cooking spray.
13. Place Air Fryer parchment paper on the bottom of the Air Fryer.
14. Preheat the Air Fryer to 380 °F (190 °C). Use the Air Fry setting and set the Preheat for 3 minutes.
15. After 30 minutes, take the churro mixture from the fridge.
16. Pipe 6, 3-inch long churro donuts onto the parchment paper in the Air Fryer drawer.
17. Set the Air Fryer for 10 minutes and use the Air Fry setting to start cooking the churros.
18. At 5 minutes, pause the Air Fryer, open the Air Fryer draw to check the churros.
19. Turn the churros over and start the Air Fryer to cook the churros for the last 5 minutes.
20. After 10 minutes, the Air Fryer will switch off. The churros should be golden brown and cooked through.
21. Repeat steps #16 to #20 until all the churros have been cooked.
22. While the churros are cooking, mix the cinnamon and sugar.
23. Melt the chocolate either in the microwave or on the stovetop.
24. Mix the melted chocolate with the cream, continue heating until the mixture is smooth and thick.
25. Remove the chocolate mixture from the microwave or stove and add the yogurt.
26. Remove the churros from the Air Fryer by using the spatula or food tongs.
27. Pour the last of the melted butter over the browned churros and sprinkle them with cinnamon and sugar.
28. Serve warm churros with chocolate sauce.

Cal: 173kcal | Carb: 12g | Fat: 11g | Prot: 3g | Sugars 6g | Fiber 1g

129. <u>**French Style Yogurt Treat**</u>

 8 to 10 minutes   6 minutes

 14 mins   4 to 5

- 1 tsp. vanilla extract
- 2 eggs, large
- 2 slices sourdough bread
- Butter as needed
- 1 to 2 teaspoon squeeze honey
- Greek yogurt for serving
- Your favorite choice of berries

1. Place your Air Fryer on a flat kitchen surface; plug it and turn it on. Set temperature to 355 °F (180 °C) and let it preheat for 4-5 minutes.
2. Take out the air-frying basket and gently coat it using a cooking oil or spray.
3. In a bowl of medium size, thoroughly whisk the vanilla and eggs. Take the bread slices and spread butter on every side. Soak them with the egg mix.

4. Add the slices to the basket. Push the air-frying basket in the Air Fryer and cook for 3 minutes.
5. Slide-out the basket; serve warm!
6. Top them with yogurt honey and berries!

Cal: 77kcal | Carb: 10g | Fat: 2g | Prot: 4g | Fiber 0g

130. <u>**Pineapple Cinnamon Treat**</u>

 8 to 10 minutes   8 minutes

 16 mins   6

- ½ tsp. baking soda
- ½ tsp. ground cinnamon
- ¼ tsp. ground anise star
- ¼ c. flaked coconut, unsweetened
- 1 pineapple, sliced
- A pinch of salt
- ½ c. water
- 2/3 c. all-purpose flour
- 1/3 c. rice flour
- ½ tsp. baking powder
- 1 c. rice milk

- ½ tp. vanilla essence
- 4 tbsp. caster sugar

1. Place your Air Fryer on a flat kitchen surface; plug it and turn it on. Set temperature to 380 °F (190 °C) and let it preheat for 4-5 minutes.
2. Take out the air-frying basket and gently coat it using a cooking oil or spray.
3. In a bowl of medium size, thoroughly mix the ingredients except for the pineapple. Coat the pineapple slices with the batter mix.
4. Add the slices to the basket. Push the air-frying basket in the Air Fryer. Cook for 8 minutes.
5. Slide-out the basket; top with the maple syrup, garnish with a dollop of vanilla ice cream.

 Cal: 178kcal | Carb: 8.4g | Fat: 1.7g | Prot: 2.6g | Fiber 1.4g

131. <u>**Plum Apple Crumble**</u>

 10 to 15 minutes   20 minutes

 30 mins   6 to 7

- 2 1/2 oz. (14 g) caster sugar
- 1/3 c. oats
- 2/3 c. flour
- ½ stick butter, chilled
- 1 tbsp. cold water
- 1 tbsp. honey
- ½ tsp. ground mace
- ¼-lb. plums, pitted and chopped
- ¼-lb. apples, cored and chopped
- 1 tbsp. lemon juice
- ½ tsp. vanilla paste
- 1 c. cranberries

1. Place your Air Fryer on a flat kitchen surface; plug it and turn it on. Set temperature to 390 °F (200 °C) and let it preheat for 4-5 minutes.
2. Take out the cake pan and gently coat it using cooking oil or spray.
3. In a bowl of medium size, thoroughly mix the plums, apples, lemon juice, sugar, honey, and mace. Add the fruit mixture to the bottom of a cake pan.
4. In a bowl of medium size, thoroughly mix the remaining ingredients and top with the fruit mix.
5. Push the air-frying basket in the Air Fryer and cook for 20 minutes.
6. Slide-out the basket; serve warm!

Cal: 188kcal | Carb: 27.8g | Fat: 8g | Prot: 1.6g | Fiber 6.3g

132. <u>**Creamy Banana Puffs**</u>

 10 to 15 minutes   10 minutes

20 mins   8

- 4 oz. (110 g) instant vanilla pudding
- 4 oz. (110 g) cream cheese, softened
- 1 package (8-oz. (230 g)) crescent dinner rolls, refrigerated
- 1 c. milk
- 2 bananas, sliced
- 1 egg, lightly beaten

1. Place your Air Fryer on a flat kitchen surface; plug it and turn it on. Set temperature to 355 °F (180 °C) and let it preheat for 4-5 minutes.
2. Unroll crescent dinner rolls and make 8 squares.
3. In a bowl of medium size, thoroughly mix the pudding and milk; whisk in the cream cheese.
4. Add the mixture to the pastry squares. Top with the slices of banana. Fold them over the filling, pressing the edges to seal. Brush each pastry puff with the whisked egg.
5. Add them to the basket. Push the air-frying basket in the Air Fryer and cook for 10 minutes.
6. Slide-out the basket; serve warm!

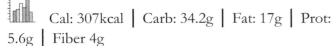 Cal: 307kcal | Carb: 34.2g | Fat: 17g | Prot: 5.6g | Fiber 4g

133. **Tasty Banana Cake**

 20 minutes   20 minutes

 40 mins   4

- 1 tsp. of baking powder
- 1 egg
- 1 c. of flour
- 1 tbsp. of soft butter
- 1 peeled banana
- ½ tsp. of cinnamon powder
- 1/3 c. of brown sugar
- Cooking spray
- 2 tbsp. of honey

1. Grease a cake pan with cooking spray.
2. Add honey, flour, and sugar to a bowl. Add banana, cinnamon, whisk, and baking powder. Mix thoroughly.
3. Pour the mixture into the greased cake pan.
4. Set the Air Fryer to 350°F. Cook for 30 minutes.
5. Serve the banana cake hot or let it cool down before serving.

 Cal: 230kcal | Carb: 1.2g | Fat: 5g | Prot: 4.3g

 Cal: 124kcal | Carb: 26.5g | Fat: 2g | Prot: 0g | Sugar 4g

134. <u>**Apple Dumplings**</u>

135. <u>**Air Fryer Chocolate Cake**</u>

 15 minutes   25 minutes

 40 mins   4

- 2 tbsp. melted coconut oil
- 2 puff pastry sheets
- 1 tbsp. brown sugar
- 2 tbsp. raisins
- 2 small apples of choice

1. Ensure your Air Fryer is preheated to 356 °F (180 °C) .
2. Core and peel apples and mix with raisins and sugar.
3. Place a bit of apple mixture into puff pastry sheets and brush sides with melted coconut oil.
4. Place into the Air Fryer. Cook 25 minutes, turning halfway through. It will be golden when done.

 5 minutes   35 minutes

 40 mins   8-10

- ½ c. hot water
- 1 tsp. vanilla
- ¼ c. olive oil
- ½ c. almond milk
- 1 egg
- ½ tsp. salt
- ¾ tsp. baking soda
- ¾ tsp. baking powder
- ½ c. unsweetened cocoa powder
- 2 c. almond flour
- 1 c. brown sugar

1. Preheat your Air Fryer to 356 °F (180 °C) .
2. Stir all dry ingredients together. Then stir in wet ingredients. Add hot water last.

3. The batter will be thin, no worries.
4. Pour cake batter into a pan that fits into the fryer. Cover with foil and poke holes into the foil.
5. Bake 35 minutes.
6. Discard foil and then bake another 10 minutes.

 Cal: 378kcal | Carb: 70.3g | Fat: 9g | Prot: 4g | Sugar 5g

136. **Apple Hand Pies**

 5 mins   8 mins

 13 mins   **6**

- 15-oz. (430 g) no-sugar-added apple pie filling
- 1 store-bought crust

1. Layout pie crust and slice into equal-sized squares.
2. Place 2 tbsp. filling into each square and seal crust with a fork.

---

3. Place into the Air Fryer. Cook 8 minutes at 390 degrees until golden in color.

 CaloriesFat: 278g | Prot: 10g | Sugar 5g

137. **Blueberry Lemon Muffins**

 10 mins   10 mins

 20 mins   12

- 1 tsp. vanilla
- Juice and zest of 1 lemon
- 2 eggs
- 1 c. blueberries
- ½ c. cream
- ¼ c. avocado oil
- ½ c. monk fruit
- 2 ½ c. almond flour

1. Mix monk fruit and flour together.
2. In another bowl, mix vanilla, egg, lemon juice, and cream together. Add mixtures together and blend well.
3. Spoon batter into cupcake holders.

4. Place in Air Fryer.
5. Bake 10 minutes at 320 °F (160 °C), checking at 6 minutes to ensure you don't overbake them.

 Cal: 317kcal | Carb: 51.5g | Fat: 11g | Prot: 3g | Sugar 5g

138. <u>**Sweet Cream Cheese Wontons**</u>

 10 mins

5 minutes

 15 mins

 16–20

- 1 egg mixed with a bit of water
- Wonton wrappers
- 1/2 c. powdered erythritol
- 8 oz. (230 g) softened cream cheese
- Olive oil

1. Mix sweetener and cream cheese together.
2. Lay out 4 wontons at a time and cover with a dish towel to prevent drying out.
3. Place ½ of a teaspoon of cream cheese mixture into each wrapper.
4. Dip finger into egg/water mixture and fold diagonally to form a triangle. Seal edges well.
5. Repeat with remaining ingredients.
6. Place filled wontons into Air Fryer and cook for 5 minutes at 400 °F (200 °C), shaking halfway through cooking.

Cal: 303kcal | Carb: 68.5g | Fat: 3g | Prot: 0.5g | Sugar 4g

139. <u>Sweet Potato Croquettes</u>

 10 minutes   10 minutes

 20 mins   4

- 2 cups mashed sweet potatoes
- ½ c. freshly grated Asiago cheese
- 1 egg, plus 1 egg yolk
- 2 tbsp. flour, divided
- 1 tbsp. fresh thyme, chopped
- ½ tsp. nutmeg
- 1 tsp. salt
- 1 tsp. black pepper
- ½ c. seasoned bread crumbs

1. Set the Air Fryer to 390 °F (200 °C) .
2. In a bowl, combine the mashed sweet potatoes, Asiago cheese, egg yolk, 1 tablespoon of the flour, thyme, nutmeg, salt, and black pepper.

3. Take heaping spoonfuls of the mixture and, using your hands, form golf ball-sized mounds.
4. Dust each one with the remaining flour.
5. Lightly beat the remaining egg and coat each croquette with it before rolling it in the seasoned bread crumbs.
6. Place the croquettes in the Air Fryer and cook, working in batches if necessary, for 8-9 minutes.
7. Remove the croquettes from the Air Fryer and serve with your favorite dipping sauce, if desired.

Cal: 275kcal | Carb: 33.6g | Fat: 10.1g | Prot: 12.7g | Saturated Fat 5.6g | Fiber 4.1g | Sugars 9.4g

140. <u>Roasted Caprese Stacks</u>

 10 minutes   15 minutes

 25 mins   4

- 2 cups heirloom tomatoes, sliced thick
- 1 c. fresh mozzarella cheese, sliced thin
- ¼ c. fresh basil, chopped
- 1 tsp. salt
- 1 tsp. black pepper
- 2 tbsp. balsamic vinegar
- 1 tbsp. olive oil

1. Set the Air Fryer to 390 °F (200 °C) .
2. Begin by dividing the tomatoes into groups of three slices.
3. Place one tomato from each group onto a baking sheet.
4. Top each with mozzarella cheese, a drizzle of balsamic vinegar, and a sprinkling of salt and black pepper.
5. Top each with an additional piece of tomato.
6. Next, add the remaining cheese, fresh basil, and any remaining balsamic vinegar, salt, and black pepper.
7. Top each with the last piece of tomato from each group.
8. Brush each stack lightly with olive oil.
9. Carefully place the stacks in the basket of the Air Fryer.
10. Cook for 12-15 minutes.

Cal: 121kcal | Carb: 5g | Fat: 8.3g | Prot: 7.6g | Saturated Fat 3.4g | Fiber 1.0g | Sugars 0.0g

141. <u>Chili Tomatoes</u>

 5 minutes   20 minutes

 25 mins   4

- 1 lb. cherry tomatoes, halved
- ¼ tsp. rosemary, dried
- 1 tsp. chili powder
- ½ c. balsamic vinegar
- 2 tbsp. olive oil
- A pinch of salt and black pepper

1. In your multi-level Air Fryer's basket, combine the tomatoes with the other ingredients and toss.

Put the basket in the instant pot, seal with Air Fryer lid and cook on Air fry mode at 400 °F (200 °C) for 20 minutes

Calories 173 | Fat: 4 g | Fiber: 2 g | Carbs: 4 g | Protein: 8 g

142. <u>Garlic Potato Mix</u>

 5 minutes   30 minutes

 35 mins   4

- 2 lb. sweet potatoes
- 1 c. bacon, cooked and chopped
- 2 tbsp. olive oil
- 1 tsp. sweet paprika
- 4 garlic cloves, minced
- Juice of 1 lime

1. In the multi-level Air Fryer's pan, combine the potatoes with the other ingredients and toss.
2. Put the pan in the instant pot and seal with the Air Fryer lid.

Cook on Roast mode at 390 °F (200 °C) for 30 minutes.

 Cal: 172kcal | Carb: 5g | Fat: 6g | Prot: 8g | Fiber 2g

143. <u>Creamy Artichokes</u>

 5 minutes   20 minutes

 25 mins   4

- 2 cups artichoke hearts, drained and halved
- 2 tbsp. butter, melted
- 2 tbsp. mustard
- 3 garlic cloves, minced
- ½ c. heavy cream

1. In the multi-level Air Fryer's pan, combine the artichokes with the other ingredients and toss.
2. Put the pan in the instant pot and seal with the Air Fryer lid.

Cook on Roast mode at 400 °F (200 °C) for 20 minutes.

Cal: 162kcal | Carb: 6g | Fat: 4g | Prot: 9g | Fiber 4g

144. <u>Cayenne Beets</u>

 5 minutes   20 minutes

 25 mins   4

- 1 lb. red beets, peeled and roughly cubed
- A pinch of salt and black pepper
- 1 tbsp. lemon zest, grated
- 1 tsp. cayenne pepper
- 1 tsp. chili pepper
- 2 tbsp. avocado oil
- Juice of 1 lemon

1. In the multi-level Air Fryer's basket, combine the beets with the other ingredients and toss.
2. Put the basket in the instant pot and seal with the Air Fryer lid.

Cook on Air fry mode at 390 °F (200 °C) for 20 minutes.

Cal: 175kcal | Carb: 4g | Fat: 5g | Prot: 8g | Fiber 2g

145. <u>Parmesan Cauliflower</u>

 15 minutes   15 minutes

 30 mins   5

- 8 cups small cauliflower florets (about 1 1/4 pounds (570 g))
- 3 tbsp. olive oil
- 1 tsp. garlic powder
- ½ tsp. salt
- ½ tsp. turmeric
- ¼ c. shredded Parmesan cheese

1. In a bowl, combine the cauliflower florets, olive oil, garlic powder, salt, turmeric, and toss to coat. Transfer to the Air Fryer basket.
2. Select "Air Fry" temperature to 390 °F (199 °C), and set time to 15 minutes.
3. After 5 minutes, remove, then stir the cauliflower florets. Return to the oven and continue cooking.
4. After 6 minutes, remove and stir the cauliflower again. Return and cook again for 4 minutes. The cauliflower florets should be crisp-tender.

5. Sprinkle with the shredded Parmesan cheese and toss well.

 Cal: 58kcal | Carb: 6g | Fat: 3g | Prot: 3g

146. Jalapeno Spinach Dip

 10 minutes   30 minutes

 40 mins   6

- 10 oz. (280 g) frozen spinach, thawed and drained
- 2 tsp. jalapeno pepper, minced
- ½ c. cheddar cheese, shredded
- 8 oz. (230 g) cream cheese
- 1/2 c. onion, diced
- 2 tsp. garlic, minced
- ½ c. mozzarella cheese, shredded
- ½ c. Monterey jack cheese, shredded
- ½ tsp. salt

1. Fit the Air Fryer with the rack in position 1.
2. Add all ingredients into the mixing bowl and mix until well combined.

3. Pour mixture into the 1-quart casserole dish.
4. Set to bake at 350 °F (180 °C) for 35 minutes. After 5 minutes, place the casserole dish in the preheated oven.
5. Serve and enjoy.

Cal: 228kcal | Carb: 4.2g | Fat: 19.8g | Prot: 9.7g | Sugar 0.8g | Cholesterol 61mg

147. Flavorful Crab Dip

 10 minutes   15 minutes

 25 mins   6

- 6 oz. (170 g) crab lump meat
- 1 tbsp. mayonnaise
- ⅛ tsp. paprika
- ¼ c. sour cream
- 4 tsp. bell pepper, diced
- 1 tbsp. butter, softened
- 1 tsp. parsley, chopped
- 1 tbsp. green onion, sliced
- ¼ c. mozzarella cheese, shredded
- 4 tsp. onion, chopped
- 2 oz. (57 g) cream cheese, softened

- ¼ tsp. salt

1. Fit the Air Fryer with the rack in position 1.
2. In a bowl, mix together cream cheese, butter, sour cream, and mayonnaise until smooth.
3. Add remaining ingredients and stir well.
4. Pour the mixture into the greased baking dish.
5. Set to bake at 350 °F (180 °C) for 20 minutes. After 5 minutes, place the baking dish in the preheated oven.
6. Serve and enjoy.

Cal: 131kcal | Carb: 8.1g | Fat: 10.8g | Prot: 6.4g | Sugar 4.3g | Cholesterol 37mg

148. <u>Spicy Brussels sprouts</u>

- ¼ tsp. garlic powder
- ¼ c. olive oil
- ¼ tsp. salt

1. Fit the Air Fryer Oven with the rack in position 1.
2. Add all ingredients into the large bowl & toss well.
3. Transfer Brussels sprouts on an Air Fryer.
4. Set to bake at 400 °F (200 °C) for 40 minutes. After 5 minutes, place the Air Fryer in the preheated oven.
5. Serve and enjoy.

Cal: 86kcal | Carb: 3g | Fat: 8.6g | Prot: 1.1g | Sugar 0.7g | Cholesterol 0mg

149. <u>Garlicky Cauliflower Florets</u>

 10 minutes 35 minutes

 45 mins 6

- 2 cups Brussels sprouts, halved
- ¼ tsp. cayenne pepper
- ½ tsp. smoked paprika
- ¼ tsp. chili powder

 10 minutes 20 minutes

 30 mins 4

- 5 cups cauliflower florets
- ½ tsp. cumin powder

- ½ tsp. ground coriander
- 6 garlic cloves, chopped
- 4 tbsp. olive oil
- ½ tsp. salt

1. Add cauliflower florets and remaining Ingredients into the large mixing bowl and toss well.
2. Add cauliflower florets into the Air Fryer basket & cook at 400 °F (200 °C) for 20 minutes. Shake basket halfway through.
3. Serve and enjoy.

Cal: 159kcal | Carb: 8.2g | Fat: 14.2g | Prot: 2.8g | Sugar 3.1g | Cholesterol 0mg

150. **Parmesan Brussels Sprouts**

 10 minutes   12 minutes

 22 mins   4

- 1 lb. Brussels sprouts, remove stems and halved

- ¼ cup parmesan cheese, grated
- 2 tbsp. olive oil
- Pepper
- Salt

1. Preheat the cosori Air Fryer to 350 °F (180 °C) .
2. In a mixing bowl, toss Brussels sprouts with oil, pepper, and salt.
3. Transfer Brussels sprouts into the Air Fryer basket and cook for 12 minutes. Shake basket halfway through.
4. Sprinkle with parmesan cheese and serve.

Cal: 129kcal | Carb: 10.6g | Fat: 8.7g | Prot: 5.9g | Sugar 2.5g | Cholesterol 4mg

151. **Flavorful Tomatoes**

 10 minutes   15 minutes

 25 mins   4

- 4 Roma tomatoes, sliced, remove seeds pithy portion
- 1 tbsp. olive oil

- ½ tsp. dried thyme
- 2 garlic cloves, minced
- Pepper
- Salt

1. Preheat the Air Fryer to 390 °F (200 °C) .
2. Toss sliced tomatoes with oil, thyme, garlic, pepper, and salt.
3. Arrange sliced tomatoes into the Air Fryer basket and cook for 15 minutes.
4. Serve and enjoy.

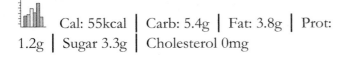 Cal: 55kcal | Carb: 5.4g | Fat: 3.8g | Prot: 1.2g | Sugar 3.3g | Cholesterol 0mg

152. **Healthy Roasted Carrots**

 10 minutes   12 minutes

 22 mins   4

- 2 cups carrots, peeled and chopped
- 1 tsp. cumin
- 1 tbsp. olive oil
- ¼ fresh coriander, chopped

1. Toss carrots with cumin and oil and place them into the Air Fryer basket.
2. Cook at 390 °F (200 °C) for 12 minutes.
3. Garnish with fresh coriander and serve.

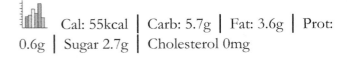 Cal: 55kcal | Carb: 5.7g | Fat: 3.6g | Prot: 0.6g | Sugar 2.7g | Cholesterol 0mg

153. **Curried Cauliflower with Pine Nuts**

 10 minutes   10 minutes

 20 mins   4

- 1 small cauliflower head, cut into florets
- 2 tbsp. olive oil
- ¼ cup pine nuts, toasted
- 1 tbsp. curry powder
- ¼ tsp. salt

1. Preheat the Air Fryer to 350 °F (180 °C) .
2. In a mixing bowl, toss cauliflower florets with oil, curry powder, and salt.

3. Add cauliflower florets into the Air Fryer basket & cook for 10 minutes. Shake basket halfway through.
4. Transfer cauliflower into the serving bowl. Add pine nuts and toss well.
5. Serve and enjoy.

Cal: 139kcal | Carb: 5.5g | Fat: 13.1g | Prot: 2.7g | Sugar 1.9g | Cholesterol 0mg

154. **Thyme Sage Butternut Squash**

 10 minutes   12 minutes

 22 mins   4

- 2 lbs. butternut squash, cut into chunks
- 1 tsp. fresh thyme, chopped
- 1 tbsp. fresh sage, chopped
- 1 tbsp. olive oil
- Pepper
- Salt

1. Preheat the Air Fryer to 390 °F (200 °C) .

---

2. In a mixing bowl, toss butternut squash with thyme, sage, oil, pepper, and salt.
3. Add butternut squash into the Air Fryer basket and cook for 10 minutes. Shake basket well & cook for 2 minutes more.
4. Serve & enjoy.

Cal: 50kcal | Carb: 4.2g | Fat: 3.8g | Prot: 1.4g | Sugar 2.5g | Cholesterol 0mg

155. **Easy Coconut Shrimp**

 10 minutes   8 minutes

 18 mins   8

- 2 eggs, lightly beaten
- 1 lb. large shrimp, peeled and deveined
- 1 cup unsweetened flaked coconut
- ¼ cup coconut flour

1. In a small bowl, add coconut flour.
2. In a shallow bowl, add eggs. In a separate shallow bowl, add flakes coconut.
3. Coat shrimp with coconut flour, then dip in eggs, and finally coat with flaked coconut.

4. Spray Air Fryer basket with cooking spray.
5. Place coated shrimp into the Air Fryer basket and cook at 400 °F (200 °C) for 6-8 minutes. Turn shrimp halfway through.

 Cal: 112kcal │ Carb: 5.1g │ Fat: 4.8g │ Prot: 12.9g │ Sugar 0.7g │ Cholesterol 122mg

156. Shrimp & Vegetable Dinner

 10 minutes 10 minutes

 20 mins 4

- 1 lb. jumbo shrimp, cleaned & peeled
- 2 tbsp. olive oil
- 1 bell pepper, cut into 1-inch pieces
- 8 oz yellow squash, sliced into ¼-inch half moons
- 1 medium zucchini, sliced into ¼-inch half moons
- 6 oz sausage, cooked and sliced
- 1 tbsp. Cajun seasoning
- ¼ tsp. salt

1. Add shrimp and remaining ingredients into the large mixing bowl and toss well to coat.
2. Preheat the cosori Air Fryer to 400 °F (200 °C) .
3. Add shrimp mixture into the Air Fryer basket and cook for 10 minutes.
4. Shake Air Fryer basket 3 times.

Cal: 312kcal │ Carb: 5.8g │ Fat: 19.3g │ Prot: 30.1g │ Sugar 5.4g │ Cholesterol 269mg

BONUS
FAST RECIPES

APPETIZERS

157. <u>Spiced Almonds</u>

 5 minutes   10 minutes

 15 mins   4

- ½ tsp. ground cinnamon
- ½ tsp. smoked paprika
- 1 c. almonds
- 1 egg white
- Sea salt to taste

1. Preheat Air Fryer to 310 °F (150 °C) . Grease the Air Fryer basket with cooking spray. In a bowl, beat the egg white with cinnamon and paprika and stir in almonds.
2. Spread the almonds on the bottom of the frying basket and Air Fry for 12 minutes,

shaking once or twice. Remove and sprinkle with sea salt to serve.

 Cal: 90kcal | Carb: 3g | Fat: 2g | Prot: 5g

158. <u>Roasted Coconut Carrots</u>

 5 minutes   10 minutes

 15 mins   4

- 1 tbsp. coconut oil, melted
- 1 lb. horse carrots, sliced
- Salt and black pepper to taste
- ½ tsp. chili powder

1. Preheat the Air Fryer to 400 °F (200 °C) .
2. Combine the carrots, coconut oil, chili powder, salt, and pepper in a mixing bowl. Place in an Air Fryer & cook for 7 minutes on high. Cook for another 5 minutes, shaking

the basket occasionally, until golden brown.
Serve.

 Cal: 80kcal | Carb: 3g | Fat: 1g | Prot: 4g

159. Crispy Kale Chips

 5 minutes   10 minutes

 15 mins   4

- 4 cups kale leaves, stems removed, chopped
- 2 tbsp. olive oil
- 1 tsp. garlic powder
- Salt and black pepper to taste
- ¼ tsp. onion powder

1. In a bowl, mix kale and olive oil. Add in garlic and onion powders, salt, and black pepper; toss to coat.
2. Arrange the kale in the frying basket and air Fry for 8 minutes at 350 °F (180 °C) , shaking once. Serve cool.

in: 8.5 g | Cholesterol: 5 mg

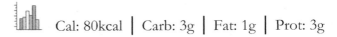 Cal: 80kcal | Carb: 3g | Fat: 1g | Prot: 3g

BREAKFAST

160. Grilled Cheese Sandwich

 5 minutes   4 minutes

 9 mins   2

- 4 Texas toast slices
- 4 Colby jack cheese slices

1. Spray Air Fryer oven tray with cooking spray.
2. Place two toast slices on a tray, then top with cheese slices.
3. Now place remaining toast slices on top of the cheese.

Air fry at 400 °F (200 °C) for 4 minutes.

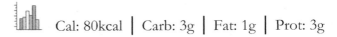 Cal: 225kcal | Fat: 4g | Saturated Fat 38.5g | Sugar 4g

161. <u>Garlic Lime Tortilla Chips</u>

 2 minutes   7 minutes

 9 mins   4

- 4 corn tortillas
- ½ teaspoon garlic granules
- ½ teaspoon salt
- 2 and ½ teaspoon fresh lime juice
- Cooking oil spray as needed

1. Preheat your Air Fryer to 347 °F (180 °C)
2. Cut tortilla into quarters and transfer to a medium bowl
3. Add garlic, salt and lime juice, toss well
4. Spray cooking basket with oil and transfer tortilla to basket, roast for 3 minutes
5. Remove the basket and spray with oil, cook for 2 minutes, repeat the process one more time until they show a golden-brown texture

 Cal: 35kcal | Carb: 7g | Fat: 0g | Prot: 3g

162. <u>Tamari Shishito Pepper</u>

 2 minutes   9 minutes

 11 mins   4

- 1/2 pound (230 g) Shishito peppers
- Olive oil as needed
- 1 tablespoon tamari
- 2 teaspoons fresh lime juice
- 2 large garlic cloves, pressed

1. Preheat your Air Fryer to 392 °F (200 °C)
2. Add pepper to your Air Fryer cooking basket and spray gently with oil
3. Roast for 3 minutes
4. While cooking, take a bowl and add lime juice, tamari, and garlic
5. Remove the basket and shake, spray with oil, and roast for 3 minutes more
6. Transfer roasted peppers to tamari mix and toss well

 Cal: 35kcal | Carb: 7g | Fat: 0g | Prot: 3g

MEAT

163. Quick & Easy Steak Tips

 10 minutes 6 minutes

 16 mins 3

- 1 ½ lb. steak, cut into ¾-inch cubes
- ⅛ tsp. cayenne
- 1 tsp. Montreal steak seasoning
- ½ tsp. garlic powder
- 1 tsp. olive oil

1. Spray Air Fryer basket with cooking spray.
2. Preheat the cosori Air Fryer to 400 °F (200 °C).
3. Toss steak cubes with oil, cayenne, steak season in garlic powder, pepper, and salt.
4. Add steak cubes into the Air Fryer basket and cook for 4-6 minutes.

Cal: 469kcal │ Carb: 0.4g │ Fat: 12.9g │ Prot: 82g │ Sugar 0.1g │ Cholesterol 204mg

164. Steak and Vegetable Kebabs

 15 minutes 5 to 7 minutes

 20 mins 2

- 2 tbsp. balsamic vinegar
- 2 tsp. olive oil
- ½ tsp. marjoram, dried
- ⅛ tsp. freshly ground black pepper
- ¾ lb. round steak, cut into 1-inch pieces
- 1 red bell pepper, sliced
- 16 button mushrooms
- 1 c. cherry tomatoes

1. In a medium bowl, stir the balsamic vinegar, olive oil, marjoram, and black pepper.
2. Add the steak and stir to coat. Let stand for 10 minutes at room temperature.
3. Alternating items, thread the beef, red bell pepper, mushrooms, and tomatoes onto 8 bamboos (see Tip, here) or metal skewers that fit in the Air Fryer.

4. Grill in the Air Fryer for 5 to 7 minutes, or until the beef is browned & reaches at least 145 °F (60 °C) on a meat thermo-meter.

5. Serve immediately.

 Cal: 194kcal | Carb: 7g | Fat: 6g | Prot: 31g | Saturated Fat 2g | Sodium 53mg | Fiber: 2 g | Sugar: 2 g

FISH

165. Cajun Shrimp

 5 minutes   5 minutes

 10 mins   6

- 560 g tiger shrimp
- 1 tbsp. olive oil
- ½ tsp. old Bay seasoning
- ¼ tsp. smoked paprika
- ¼ tsp. cayenne pepper

1. Set the Air Fryer at 390 °F (200 °C) .
2. Cover the shrimp using the oil and spices.

3. Toss them into the Air Fryer basket & set the timer for five minutes.
4. Serve with your favorite side dish.

 Cal: 356kcal | Carb: 5g | Fat: 18g | Prot: 34g

166. Easy Crab Sticks

 5 minutes   10 minutes

 15 mins   4

- 1 package Crab sticks
- Cooking oil spray, as needed

1. Take each of the sticks out of the package and unroll it until the stick is flat. Tear the sheets into thirds.
2. Arrange them on the Air Fryer basket and lightly spritz using cooking spray. Set the timer for 10 minutes.
3. Note: If you shred the crab meat, you can cut the time in half, but they will also easily fall through the holes in the basket.

Cal: 285kcal | Carb: 3.7g | Fat: 12.8g | Prot: 38.1g

VEGETABLES

167. Individual Portabella White Pizzas

 10 minutes   5 minutes

 15 mins   4

- 4 large portabella mushroom caps
- 2 teaspoons olive oil
- 1 teaspoon salt
- 1 teaspoon black pepper, coarsely ground
- ½ teaspoon rubbed sage
- ¼ c. crème fraîche
- 1 tablespoon fresh chives, chopped
- ½ c. goat cheese, crumbled
- ½ c. fresh mozzarella cheese, shredded
- ¼ c. walnuts, chopped

1. Set the Air Fryer to 325 °F (160 °C) .

2. Brush the mushroom caps with olive oil and season them with salt, black pepper, and rubbed sage.
3. Combine the crème fraîche with the chives and spread a layer on each mushroom cap.
4. Top each mushroom with goat cheese, mozzarella cheese, and walnuts.
5. Place the mushroom caps in the Air Fryer and cook for 5 minutes.

 Cal: 230kcal | Carb: 6.4g | Fat: 19.3g | Prot: 10.6g | Saturated Fat 7.9g | Fiber 3.5g | Sugars 2.2g

168. Masala Artichokes

 5 minutes   10 minutes

 15 mins   4

- 2 cups canned artichoke hearts, halved
- 1 tsp. garam masala
- 1 tsp. chili powder
- 2 tbsp. olive oil
- A pinch of salt and black pepper
- 2 tbsp. balsamic vinegar
- 1 tbsp. dill, chopped

1. In the multi-level Air Fryer's pan, combine the beef with the other ingredients and toss.
2. Put the pan in the instant pot and seal with the Air Fryer lid.

Cook on Roast mode at 400 °F (200 °C) for 30 minutes.

 Cal: 200kcal | Carb: 3g | Fat: 6g | Prot: 6g | Fiber 2g

SNACKS

169. Chimichanga

 2 minutes   8 minutes

 10 mins   1

- 1 whole-grain tortilla
- ½ c. vegan refried beans
- ¼ c. grated vegan cheese (optional)
- Cooking oil spray (sunflower, safflower)
- ½ c. fresh salsa (or Green Chili Sauce)
- 2 cups chopped romaine lettuce (about ½ head)
- Guacamole (optional)
- Chopped cilantro (optional)
- Cheesy Sauce (optional)

1. Lay the tortilla on a flat surface and place the beans in the center. Top with the cheese, if using.
2. Wrap the bottom up over the filling, and then fold in the sides. Then roll it all up to enclose the beans inside the tortilla (you're making an enclosed burrito here).
3. Spray the Air Fryer basket with oil, place the tortilla wrap inside the basket, seam-side down, and spray the top of the chimichanga with oil.
4. Fry for 5 minutes. Spray the top (and sides) again with oil, flip over, and spray the other side with oil. Fry for an additional 2 or 3 minutes, until nicely browned and crisp.
5. Transfer to a plate. Top with the salsa, lettuce, guacamole, cilantro, and/or Cheesy Sauce, if using. Serve immediately.

 Cal: 317kcal | Carb: 55g | Fat: 6g | Prot: 13g

170. Kale Chips Vegan-Friendly

 5 minutes 7 minutes

 12 mins 2

- 1 bunch curly kale
- 2 tsp. olive oil
- 1 tbsp. nutritional yeast
- ⅛ tsp. black pepper
- ¼ tsp. sea salt

1. Warm the Air Fryer unit to reach 390 °F (200 °C).
2. Thoroughly rinse the kale and pat it dry. Remove the leaves from the stems of the kale and toss them into a mixing container.
3. Add the olive oil, salt, pepper, and nutritional yeast. Use your hands to massage the toppings into the kale leaves.
4. Scoop the kale into the basket of the fryer— air-fry them until they are crispy (6-7 min.).
5. Note: If you are using a small Air Fryer, cook the chips in two batches. You don't want to overfill the fryer basket.
6. Enjoy them piping hot or slightly cooled.

7. Save any leftover chips in a zip-top bag for up to five days.

 Cal: 90kcal | Carb: 9.1g | Fat: 4.3g | Prot: 3.8g | Fat Content 5.3g

171. Whole-Wheat Air-Fried Pizzas

 5 minutes 10 minutes

 15 mins 2

- ¼ c. lower-sodium marinara sauce
- 2 whole-wheat pita rounds
- 1 c. baby spinach leaves
- 1 small plum tomato
- 1 small garlic clove
- ¼ c. pre-shredded part-skim mozzarella cheese
- 1 tbsp. shaved Parmigiano-Regiano cheese

1. Warm the Air Fryer to 350 °F (180 °C).
2. Spread the marinara sauce over one side of each pita bread.

3. Slice the tomato into eight slices and thinly slice the garlic.
4. Top each one-off using half of the spinach leaves, tomato slices, garlic, and cheeses.
5. Place one pita in the fryer basket, and air-fry it until the cheese is melted and the pita is crispy (4-5 min.).
6. Repeat with the remaining pita and serve.

 Cal: 229kcal │ Carb: 37g │ Fat: 4.1g │ Prot: 11g │ Fat Content 5g

SAUCES

172. Chicken and Black Olives Sauce

 10 min   8 min

 18 mins   2

- 1 chicken breast cut into 4 pieces
- 2 tbsp. olive oil
- 3 garlic cloves, minced

For the sauce:
- 1 c. black olives, pitted
- Salt and black pepper to the taste
- 2 tbsp. olive oil
- ¼ c. parsley, chopped
- 1 tbsp. lemon juice

1. In your food processor, mix olives with salt, pepper, 2 tablespoons olive oil, lemon juice, and parsley, blend very well and transfer to a bowl.
2. Season chicken with salt and pepper, rub with the oil and garlic, place in your preheated Air Fryer, and cook at 370 °F (190 °C) for 8 minutes.
3. Divide chicken on plates, top with olives sauce and serve.

 Cal: 270kcal │ Carb: 23g │ Fat: 12g │ Prot: 22g │ Fiber 12g

DESSERTS

173. Poached Up Carrots

 5 minutes   5 minutes

 10 mins   4

- 2 lb. carrots
- Pepper as needed
- 1 c. of water
- 1 tbsp. coconut butter

1. Wash carrots thoroughly & peel them, slice the carrots.
2. Add carrots, water to the Air Fryer.
3. Lock pressure lid & cook for 4 minutes on HIGH pressure.
4. Release pressure naturally.
5. Strain carrots and strain carrots.
6. Mix with coconut butter, enjoy with a bit of pepper.

Cal: 228kcal | Carb: 36g | Fat: 8g | Prot: 4g | Saturated Fat 2g | Fiber 2g | Sodium 123mg

174. <u>**Easy Air Fryer Donuts**</u>

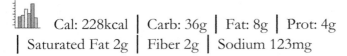

- Pinch of allspice
- 4 tbsp. dark brown sugar
- ½ - 1 tsp. cinnamon
- 1/3 c. granulated sweetener
- 3 tbsp. melted coconut oil
- 1 can of biscuits

1. Mix allspice, sugar, sweetener, and cinnamon together.
2. Take out biscuits from the can and with a circle cookie cutter, cut holes from centers, and place into Air Fryer.
3. Cook 5 minutes at 350 °F (180 °C) . As batches are cooked, use a brush to coat with melted coconut oil and dip each into a sugar mixture.
4. Serve warm!

Cal: 209kcal | Carb: 43.3g | Fat: 4g | Prot: 0g | Sugar 3g

175. <u>**Perfect Cinnamon Toast**</u>

 5 mins   5 mins

 10 mins   8

 5 minutes   5 minutes

 10 mins   6

- 2 tsp. pepper
- 1 ½ tsp. vanilla extract
- 1 ½ tsp. cinnamon
- ½ c. sweetener of choice
- 1 c. coconut oil
- 12 slices whole-wheat bread

1. Melt coconut oil and mix with sweetener until dissolved. Mix in remaining ingredients minus bread till incorporated.

2. Spread mixture onto bread, covering all area. Place coated pieces of bread in your Air Fryer.
3. Cook 5 minutes at 400 °F (200 °C) .
4. Remove and cut diagonally.
5. Enjoy!

Cal: 124kcal | Carb: 26.5g | Fat: 2g | Prot: 0g | Sugar 4g

BONUS
GLUTEN-FREE RECIPES

APPETIZERS

176. <u>Simple Buttered Potatoes</u>

 5 minutes   30 minutes

 35 mins   4

-
- **1-pound (450 g) potatoes, cut into** wedges
- 2 garlic cloves, grated
- 1 tsp. fennel seeds
- 2 tbsp. butter, melted
- Salt and black pepper to taste

1. Mix the potatoes, butter, garlic, fennel seeds, salt, and black pepper in a mixing bowl until thoroughly combined. In the Air Fryer basket, arrange the potatoes.
2. Bake for 25 minutes at 360 °F (180 °C) , shaking once halfway through, until crispy on

the exterior and soft on the inside. Warm the dish before serving.

 Cal: 100kcal | Carb: 8g | Fat: 4g | Prot: 7g

177. <u>Corn-Crusted Chicken Tenders</u>

 10 minutes   25 minutes

 35 mins   4

- 2 chicken breasts, cut into strips
- Salt and black pepper to taste
- 2 eggs
- 1 c. ground cornmeal

1. Preheat Air Fryer to 390 °F (200 °C) .
2. In a bowl, mix ground cornmeal, salt, and black pepper. In another bowl, beat the eggs; season w/ salt and pepper. Dip the chicken

in the eggs and then coat in cornmeal. Spray the prepared sticks with cooking spray and place them in the Air Fryer basket in a single layer. Air Fry for 6 minutes, slide the basket out, and flip the sticks; cook for 6-8 more minutes until golden brown.

 Cal: 170kcal | Carb: 8g | Fat: 6g | Prot: 16g

178. Duck Fat Roasted Red Potatoes

 5 minutes   25 minutes

 30 mins   4

- 4 red potatoes, cut into wedges
- 1 tbsp. garlic powder
- Salt and black pepper to taste
- 2 tbsp. thyme, chopped
- 3 tbsp. duck fat, melted

1. Preheat Air Fryer to 380 F. In a bowl, mix duck fat, garlic powder, salt, and pepper. Add the potatoes and shake to coat.

2. Place in the basket and bake for 12 minutes, remove the basket, shake and continue cooking for another 8-10 minutes until golden brown. Serve warm topped with thyme.

 Cal: 110kcal | Carb: 8g | Fat: 5g | Prot: 7g

179. Chicken Wings with Alfredo Sauce

 5 minutes   20 minutes

 25 mins   4

- 1 ½ lb. chicken wings, pat-dried
- Salt to taste
- ½ c. Alfredo sauce

1. Preheat Air Fryer to 370 °F (190 °C) .
2. Season the wings with salt. Arrange them in the greased Air Fryer basket, without touching, and Air Fry for 12 minutes until no longer pink in the center. Work in batches if needed. Flip them, increase the heat to 390 °F (200 °C) and cook for 5 more minutes.

Plate the wings and drizzle with Alfredo sauce to serve.

 Cal: 150kcal | Carb: 7g | Fat: 5g | Prot: 14g

180. Crispy Squash

 5 minutes 20 minutes

 25 mins 4

- 2 cups butternut squash, cubed
- 2 tbsp. olive oil
- Salt and black pepper to taste
- ¼ tsp. dried thyme
- 1 tbsp. fresh parsley, finely chopped

1. In a bowl, add squash, olive oil, salt, pepper, and thyme, and toss to coat.
2. Place the squash in the Air Fryer and Air Fry for 14 minutes at 360 °F (180 °C) , shaking once or twice. Serve sprinkled with fresh parsley.

 Cal: 100kcal | Carb: 5g | Fat: 2g | Prot: 3g

181. Classic French Fries

 10 minutes 15 minutes

 25 mins 2

- 2 russet potatoes, cut into strips
- 2 tbsp. olive oil
- salt and black pepper to taste
- ½ c. aioli

1. Preheat the fryer to 400 °F (200 °C) . Spray the Air Fryer basket with cooking spray.
2. In a bowl, brush the strips with olive oil and season with salt and black pepper. Put it in the Air Fryer and cook for 20-22 minutes, turning once halfway through, until crispy. Serve with garlic aioli.

Cal: 120kcal | Carb: 7g | Fat: 4g | Prot: 6g

BREAKFAST

182. Tomato Spinach Frittata

 10 minutes   7 minutes

 17 mins   1

- 2 eggs, lightly beaten
- ¼ c. spinach, chopped
- ¼ c. tomatoes, chopped
- 2 tbsp. milk
- 1 tbsp. parmesan cheese, grated
- Pepper
- Salt

1. In a medium bowl, whisk eggs. Add remaining ingredients and whisk.
2. Spray a small Air Fryer pan with cooking spray.

Pour egg into the prepared pan and cook at 330 °F (170 °C) for 7 minutes.

Cal: 189kcal | Carb: 5.3g | Fat: 11.7g | Prot: 15.7g | Saturated Fat 4.3g | Sugar 3.3g | Cholesterol 337mg

183. Roasted Brussels Sprouts & Sweet Potatoes

 10 minutes   20 minutes

 30 mins   4

- 1 lb. Brussels sprouts, cut in half
- 2 sweet potatoes, wash, and cut into 1-inch pieces
- 2 tbsp. olive oil
- ¼ tsp. garlic powder
- ½ tsp. pepper
- 1 tsp. salt

1. Add sweet potatoes and Brussels sprouts.
2. Add remaining ingredients over sweet potatoes and Brussels sprouts and toss until well coated.
3. Transfer sweet potatoes and Brussels sprouts on an Air Fryer oven tray and roast at 40 °F (0 °C) for 10 minutes.
4. Turn sweet potatoes and Brussels sprouts to the other side and roast for 10 minutes more.

Cal: 138kcal | Carb: 13.3g | Fat: 7.4g | Prot: 4.4g | Saturated Fat 17.2g | Sugar 3.9g | Cholesterol 0mg

184. Breakfast Egg Bites

 10 minutes   13 minutes

 23 mins   4

- 4 eggs, lightly beaten
- ¼ c. ham, diced
- ¼ c. cheddar cheese, shredded
- ¼ c. bell pepper, diced
- ½ c. milk
- Pepper
- Salt

1. Add all ingredients & whisk until well combined.
2. Spray muffin silicone mold with cooking spray.
3. Pour egg mixture into the silicone muffin mold, place it in the Air Fryer oven, and bake at 350 °F (180 °C) for 10 minutes.

4. After 10 minutes, flip egg bites and cook for 3 minutes more.

 Cal: 123kcal | Carb: 2.8g | Fat: 8.1g | Prot: 9.8g | Saturated Fat 2.8g | Sugar 2.1g | Cholesterol 178mg

185. Basil Feta Egg Bite

 10 minutes   5 minutes

 15 mins   7

- 4 eggs
- 1 tbsp. fresh basil, chopped
- ¼ cup sun-dried tomatoes, diced
- ¼ cup feta cheese, crumbled
- ½ cup cottage cheese, crumbled

1. Spray egg mold with cooking spray and set aside.
2. In a bowl, beat eggs until frothy. Add remaining ingredients into the eggs and stir to mix.
3. Pour egg mixture into the egg mold.

Place egg mold into the Air Fryer basket and cook at 330 °F (170 °C) for 5 minutes.

Cal: 66kcal │ Carb: 1.3g │ Fat: 4g │ Prot: 6.2g │ Sugar 0.6g │ Cholesterol 100mg

MEAT

186. Simple Sirloin Steaks

 10 minutes   12 minutes

 22 mins   2

- 2 sirloin steaks
- 2 tbsp. steak seasoning

1. Spray steaks w/ cooking spray and season with steak seasoning.
2. Place steaks into the Air Fryer basket and cook at 400 °F (200 °C) for 12 minutes.
3. Turn steaks halfway through.

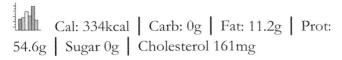 Cal: 334kcal │ Carb: 0g │ Fat: 11.2g │ Prot: 54.6g │ Sugar 0g │ Cholesterol 161mg

187. Flavorful Steak

 10 minutes   18 minutes

 28 mins   2

- 2 steaks, rinsed and pat dry with a paper towel
- 1 tsp. olive oil
- ½ tsp. garlic powder
- ¼ tsp. onion powder

1. Rub steaks with oil and season with garlic powder, onion powder, pepper, and salt.
2. Place steaks into the Air Fryer basket and cook at 400 °F (200 °C) for 18 minutes.
3. Turn steaks halfway through.

Cal: 252kcal │ Carb: 0.8g │ Fat: 8.1g │ Prot: 41.7g │ Sugar 0.3g │ Cholesterol 104mg

188. Simple Beef Sirloin Roast

 10 minutes   50 minutes

 1 h and 0 min   2

- 2½ lb. sirloin roast
- Salt and ground black pepper, as required

1. Rub the roast with salt and black pepper generously.
2. Insert the rotisserie rod through the roast.
3. Insert the rotisserie forks, one on each side of the rod to secure the rod to the chicken.
4. Arrange the drip pan in the bottom of the Air Fryer Oven cooking chamber.
5. Select "Roast" and then adjust the temperature to 350 °F (180 °C) .
6. Set the timer for 50 minutes and press the "Start".
7. When the display shows "Add Food" press the red lever down and load the left side of the rod.
8. Now, slide the rod's left side into the groove along the metal bar so it doesn't move.
9. Then, close the door and touch "Rotate".

10. When cooking time is complete, press the red lever to release the rod.
11. Remove and place the roast onto a platter for about 10 minutes before slicing.
12. With a sharp knife, cut the roast into desired-sized slices and serve.

Cal: 201kcal | Fat: 8.8g | Saturated Fat 3.1g | Cholesterol 94mg | Sodium 88mg | Total Carbs: 0 g | Fiber: 0 g | Sugar: 0 g | Protein: 28.9 g

189. Bacon-Wrapped Filet Mignon

 10 minutes   15 minutes

 25 mins   2

- 2 bacon slices
- 2 (4-oz. (110 g)) filet mignon
- Salt and ground black pepper, as required
- Olive oil cooking spray

1. Wrap 1 bacon slice around each filet mignon and secure with toothpicks.

2. Season the filets with the salt and black pepper lightly.
3. Arrange the filet mignon onto a coking rack and spray with cooking spray.
4. Arrange the drip pan in the bottom of the Air Fryer Oven cooking chamber.
5. Select "Air Fry" and then adjust the temperature to 375 °F (190 °C) .
6. Set the timer for 15 minutes and press the "Start".
7. When the display shows "Add Food" insert the cooking rack in the center position.
8. When the display shows "Turn Food" turn the filets.
9. When cooking time is complete, remove the rack and serve hot.

Cal: 360kcal | Fat: 19.6g | Saturated Fat 6.8g | Cholesterol 108mg | Sodium 737mg | Total Carbs: 0.4 g | Fiber: 0 g | Sugar: 0 g | Protein: 42.6 g

FISH

190. Crunchy Air Fryer Fish

 5 minutes   15 minutes

 20 mins   4

- 1 tsp. paprika
- ½ c. yellow cornmeal
- ½ tsp. garlic powder
- 1 large egg
- 1 tsp. coarse salt
- ½ tsp. black pepper
- 1 lb. white fish fillets
- Lemon and parsley for garnish (optional)
- Oil spray

1. Preheat the Air Fryer for 3 minutes at 400 °F (200 °C) . Beat the egg in a shallow skillet. In a different deep skillet, mix the cornmeal and spices.
2. Dry the fish completely. Drop the fish fillets in the egg; allow extra drip into the pan. Press the fish into the cornmeal combination until well-crusted on the two sides.
3. Place the coated fish in the basket of the preheated fryer. Spray lightly with oil. Cook for 10 minutes, tossing the fish to ensure uniform cooking. If there are dry spots, spray a little oil. Take back the basket to the Air Fryer and cook until the fish is well prepared.
4. Lightly squeeze with lemon and sprinkle with parsley.
5. Serve immediately.

 Cal: 191kcal | Carb: 15g | Fat: 3g | Prot: 24g

191. Buttery Cod

 5 minutes   15 minutes

 20 mins   4

- 1 tbsp. parsley, chopped
- 3 tbsp. butter, melted
- 8 cherry tomatoes, halved
- 0.25 c. tomato sauce
- 2 cod fillets, cubed

1. Turn on the Air Fryer to 390 °F (200 °C) .
2. Combine all of the ingredients and put them into a pan that works with the Air Fryer.
3. After 12 minutes of baking, you can divide this between the four bowls and enjoy.

 Cal: 232kcal | Carb: 5g | Fat: 8g | Prot: 11g

192. Grilled Sardines

 5 minutes   20 minutes

 25 mins   4

- 5 sardines
- Herbs of Provence

1. Preheat the Air Fryer to 320 °F (160 °C) .
2. Spray the basket and place your sardines in the basket of your fryer.
3. Set the timer for 14 minutes. After 7 minutes, remember to turn the sardines so that they are roasted on both sides.

 Cal: 189kcal | Carb: 0g | Fat: 10g | Prot: 22g

193. Mussels with Pepper

 15 minutes   20 minutes

 35 mins   5

- 700 g mussels
- 1 garlic clove
- 1 tsp. oil
- Pepper to taste
- Parsley to taste

1. Clean and scrape the mold cover and remove the byssus (the "beard" that comes out of the mold).
2. Pour the oil, clean the mussels and the crushed garlic in the Air Fryer basket. Set the temperature to 390 °F (200 °C) and simmer for 12 minutes. Towards the end of cooking, add black pepper and chopped parsley.
3. Finally, distribute the mussel juice well at the bottom of the basket, stirring the basket.

 Cal: 150kcal | Carb: 2g | Fat: 8g | Prot: 15g

VEGETABLES

194. Mexican Roasted Baby Carrots

 10 minutes   20 minutes

 30 mins   4

- 4 cups baby carrots
- 1 tbsp. olive oil
- 1 tsp. ground cumin
- 1 tsp. Mexican oregano
- ½ tsp. cayenne powder
- 1 tsp. salt
- 1 tsp. black pepper
- ¼ c. fresh cilantro

1. Set the Air Fryer to 390 °F (200 °C) .
2. Drizzle the carrots with the olive oil and season them with the ground cumin, Mexican oregano, cayenne powder, salt, and black pepper. Toss to mix.
3. Place the carrots in the Air Fryer and cook for 20 minutes.

4. Remove the carrots from the Air Fryer and toss them with the fresh cilantro before serving.

 Cal: 65kcal | Carb: 8g | Fat: 3.5g | Prot: 1g | Saturated Fat 0.5g | Fiber 2.0g | Sugars 4.0g

195. Chili Beet

 5 minutes   30 minutes

 35 mins   4

- 1 lb. red beets,
- 2 tbsp. avocado oil
- A pinch of salt and black pepper
- 1 tsp. chili powder
- 1 tbsp. chives, chopped
- Juice of 1 lime

1. In your multi-level Air Fryer's basket, combine the beets with the oil and the other ingredients except for the chives and toss.
Put the basket in the instant pot, seal with the Air Fryer lid and cook on Air fry mode at 400 °F (200 °C) for 30 minutes.

 Cal: 200kcal | Carb: 4g | Fat: 5g | Prot: 6g | Fiber 2g

196. Yogurt Potatoes Mix

 4 minutes   25 minutes

 29 mins   4

- 1 lb. gold potatoes, peeled & cut into wedges
- 1 tsp. turmeric powder
- 1 tsp. coriander, ground
- 2 tbsp. olive oil
- A pinch of salt and black pepper
- 1 c. Greek yogurt
- 1 c. dill, chopped
- 2 garlic cloves, minced

1. In the multi-level Air Fryer's pan, combine the potatoes with the other ingredients and toss.
2. Put the pan in the instant pot and seal with the Air Fryer lid.
3. Cook on Roast mode at 400 °F (200 °C) for 25 minutes.

146

4. Divide everything between plates and serve.

 Cal: 194kcal | Carb: 4g | Fat: 6g | Prot: 8g | Fiber 2g

SNACKS

197. Bacon-Wrapped Avocados

 10 minutes   30 minutes

 40 mins   4

- 12 thick strips of bacon
- Large avocados, sliced
- 1/3 tsp. salt
- 1/3 tsp. chili powder
- 1/3 tsp. cumin powder

1. Stretch the bacon strips to elongate and use a knife to cut in half to make 24 pieces. Wrap each bacon piece around a slice of avocado from one end to the other end. Tuck the end of bacon into the wrap. Arrange on a flat surface and season with salt, chili, and cumin on both sides.
2. Arrange 4 to 8 wrapped pieces in the Air Fryer and cook at 350 °F (180 °C) for 8 minutes, or until the bacon is browned and crunchy, flipping halfway through to cook evenly. Remove
3. Onto a wire rack and repeat the process for the remaining avocado pieces.

 Cal: 193kcal | Carb: 10g | Fat: 16g | Prot: 4g

198. Cinnamon Apple Chips with Yogurt Dip

 5 minutes   20 minutes

 25 mins   4

- 230 g apple (such as Fuji or Honeycrisp)
- 1 tsp. ground cinnamon
- 2 tsp. canola oil
- Cooking oil spray (as needed)
- ¼ c. plain 1% low-fat Greek yogurt
- 1 tsp. honey

147

- 1 tbsp. almond butter

1. Heat the Air Fryer unit to reach 375 °F (190 °C).
2. Thinly slice the apple on a mandoline. Toss the slices in a bowl with cinnamon and oil to evenly cover.
3. Spritz the fryer basket using cooking spray.
4. Arrange seven to eight sliced apples in the basket (single-layered).
5. Air-fry them for 12 minutes (flipping them every 4 min.) and rearrange slices to flatten them. They will continue to crisp upon cooling. Continue the procedure with the rest of the apple slices.
6. Whisk the yogurt with the almond butter and honey in a mixing container until smooth.
7. Arrange six to eight sliced apples on each plate with a small dollop of dipping sauce.

Cal: 104kcal | Carb: 17g | Fat: 3.6g | Prot: 1g | Fat Content 3g

SAUCES

199. **Beet Salad with Parsley Dressing**

 15 minutes   15 minutes

 30 mins   4

- Black pepper and salt
- 1 clove of garlic
- 2 tbsp. of balsamic vinegar
- 4 beets
- 2 tbsp. of capers
- 1 bunch of chopped parsley
- 1 tbsp. of olive oil

1. Place bets on the Power XL Air Fryer Grill pan.
2. Set the Power XL Air Fryer Grill to the air fry function.
3. Set Timer and temperature to 15 minutes and 360 °F (180 °C) .
4. In another bowl, mix pepper, garlic, capers, salt, and olive oil. Mix well

5. Remove the beets from the Power XL Air Fryer Grill and place them on a flat surface.
6. Peel and put it in the salad bowl
7. Serve with vinegar.

Serving Suggestions: Dress with parsley mixture.

Directions & Cooking Tips: Rinse beets before cooking.

 Cal: 185kcal │ Carb: 11g │ Fat: 16g │ Prot: 8g

200. **Onion Dip**

 10 minutes   25 minutes

 35 mins   8

- 2 lbs. onion, chopped
- ½ tsp. baking soda
- ½ tbsp. butter, softened
- Pepper Salt

1. Melt butter in a pan over medium heat.
2. Add onion and baking soda and sauté for 5 minutes.

3. Transfer the onion mixture into the Air Fryer baking dish.
4. Place in the Air Fryer and cook at 370 °F (190 °C) for 25 minutes.
5. Serve and enjoy.

 Cal: 143kcal │ Carb: 8.1g │ Fat: 9g │ Prot: 9g │ Sugar 5.7g │ Cholesterol 175mg

DESSERTS

201. **Poached Pears**

 5 minutes   10 minutes

 15 mins   6

- 6 firm pears, peeled
- 4 garlic cloves, minced
- 1 stick cinnamon
- 1 fresh ginger, minced
- 1 bottle of dry red wine
- 1 bay leaf
- Mixed Italian herbs as needed
- 1 and 1/3 cups stevia

1. Peel the pears leaving the stems attached.
2. Pour wine into your Air Fryer.
3. Add cinnamon, cloves, ginger, bay leaf, and stevia, stir gently.
4. Add pears to the pot.
5. Close the lid.
6. Cook for 9 minutes on HIGH.
7. Quickly release the pressure.
8. Take the pears out using a tong, keep them on the side.
9. Set Sauté mode, make the mixture in half.
10. Drizzle the mixture with pears.
11. Serve and enjoy!

 Cal: 150kcal | Carb: 2g | Fat: 16g | Prot: 0.5g | Saturated Fat 4g | Fiber 0g | Sodium 13mg

202. Chocolate Soufflé for Two

 15 mins   14 mins

 29 mins   2

- 2 tbsp. almond flour
- ½ tsp. vanilla
- 3 tbsp. sweetener
- 2 separated eggs
- ¼ c. melted coconut oil
- 3 oz. (85 g) of semi-sweet chocolate, chopped

1. Brush coconut oil and sweetener onto ramekins.
2. Melt coconut oil and chocolate together. Beat egg yolks well, adding vanilla and sweetener. Stir in flour and ensure there are no lumps.
3. Preheat Air Fryer to 330 °F (170 °C).
4. Whisk egg whites till they reach peak state and fold them into chocolate mixture.
5. Pour batter into ramekins and place into the fryer.
6. Cook 14 minutes.
7. Serve with powdered sugar dusted on top.

 Cal: 238kcal | Carb: 45g | Fat: 6g | Prot: 1g | Sugar 4g

MEAL PLAN

Week 1

DAY	BREAKFAST	LUNCH	DINNER
MONDAY	Tomato Spinach Frittata**Error! Bookmark not defined.**	Beef and Fruit Stir-Fry	Beef Jerky
TUESDAY	Roasted Brussels Sprouts & Sweet Potatoes	Bacon-Wrapped Filet Mignon	Crispy Mustard Pork Tenderloin
WEDNESDAY	Roasted Potato wedges	Sweet & Spicy Meatballs	Pork and Fruit Kebabs
THURSDAY	Breakfast Egg Bites	Apple Pork Tenderloin	Lamb Patties
FRIDAY	Grilled Cheese Sandwich	Spicy Grilled Steak	Glazed Pork Tenderloin
SATURDAY	Coated Avocado Tacos	Lamb Meatballs	Beef Fillet with Garlic Mayo
SUNDAY	Spiced Sweet Potato Fries	Seasoned Pork Tenderloin	Burgers Patties

Week 2

DAY	BREAKFAST	LUNCH	DINNER
MONDAY	Crispy Potato Skins	Sweet Potato Croquettes	Crunchy Air Fryer Fish
TUESDAY	Air Fryer Potato Wedges	Yogurt Potatoes Mix	Mexican Roasted Baby Carrots
WEDNESDAY	Coated Onion Rings	Roasted Caprese Stacks	Buttery Cod
THURSDAY	Balsamic-Glazed Cool Carrots	Beef Fillet with Garlic Mayo	Tender & Juicy Kebab
FRIDAY	Crazy Green Tomatoes	Chili Beet	Breaded Cod Sticks
SATURDAY	Tamari Shishito Pepper	Tasty Shrimp Fajitas	Individual Portabella White Pizzas
SUNDAY	Garlic Lime Tortilla Chips	Parmesan Cauliflower	Cajun Shrimp

Week 3

DAY	BREAKFAST	LUNCH	DINNER
MONDAY	Rosemary Flavored Potato Chips	Crispy Baked Avocado Tacos	Easy Crab Sticks
TUESDAY	Cheesed Up Vegan Fries and Shallots	Beet Salad with Parsley Dressing	BBQ Pork Chops
WEDNESDAY	Cool Berber Spiced Fries	Cheesy Beef Sandwiches	Zucchini with Tuna
THURSDAY	Miso Brussels	Asian Beef	Meatballs Surprise
FRIDAY	Spiced Up Okra		Fried Catfish
SATURDAY	Blooming Onion	Monkfish with Olives and Capers	Fresh Pizza
SUNDAY	Bacon Brussels Sprouts	Teriyaki Wings	Caramelized Salmon Fillet

CONCLUSION

Air fryer are popular nowadays due to their convenience, but you might want to consider the potential risks before purchasing one. These electric devices are not designed for cooking with oils, which means that any food cooked in an Air Fryer will likely contain liquid oils. This liquid oil can then drip out of the unit and onto your countertop or into your kitchen sink due to the design of most models.

Additionally, many Air Fryers have settings that often result in undercooked food and over-cooked food. This is because of the uneven heating element used in the cooking process. These devices are designed to produce crispy food, but they can't or won't do so based on your settings. For this reason, you should only use the Air Fryer as a convenience device for deep-frying foods.

If you plan to use the Air Fryer as a regular cooking appliance, we recommend that you purchase one with a digital display and variable temperature control. Most models use infrared technology to regulate the temperature of the heating element.

Although we believe that most users do not understand how to properly use their Air Fryer and may end up damaging it, we still recommend that you purchase an Air Fryer because of its convenience. Additionally, these devices are safer than other methods of cooking because they do not produce excessive heat or grease. Air fryers also heat faster than other traditional methods of cooking and help to save time as well as money.

Overall, if you want to buy an Air Fryer and eat healthier, as a result, go for one of those models that has a large cooking chamber. Look for one with about 9 to 10 inches (22,8 - 25,4 cm) inside it and that is designed to cook food without oils.

MEASUREMENT CONVERSION

TEMPERATURE	
FAHRENHEIT	**CELSIUS**
100 °F	37 °C
150 °F	65 °C
200 °F	93 °C
250 °F	121 °C
300 °F	150 °C
325 °F	160 °C
350 °F	180 °C
375 °F	190 °C
400 °F	200 °C
425 °F	220 °C
450 °F	230 °C
500 °F	260 °C
525 °F	270 °C
550 °F	288 °C

WEIGHT	
IMPERIAL	**METRIC**
½ oz.	15 g
1 oz.	29 g
2 oz.	57 g
3 oz.	85 g
4 oz.	113 g
5 oz.	141 g
6 oz.	170 g
8 oz.	227 g
10 oz.	283 g
12 oz.	340 g
13 oz.	369 g
14 oz.	397 g
15 oz.	425 g
1 lb.	453 g

MEASUREMENT			
CUP	**OUNCES**	**MILLILITERS**	**TABLESPOON**
1/16 c.	½ oz.	15 ml	1
⅛ c.	1 oz.	30 ml	3
¼ c.	2 oz.	59 ml	4
1/3 c.	2.5 oz.	79 ml	5.5
3/8 c.	3 oz.	90 ml	6
½ c.	4 oz.	118 ml	8
2/3 c.	5 oz.	158 ml	11
¾ c.	6 oz.	177 ml	12
1 c.	8 oz.	240 ml	16
2 c.	16 oz.	480 ml	32
4 c.	32 oz.	960 ml	64
5 c.	40 oz.	1180 ml	80
6 c.	48 oz.	1420 ml	96
8 c.	64 oz.	1895 ml	128

COOKING CHART

Vegetables					
INGREDIENT	AMOUNT	PREPARATION	OIL	TEMP	COOK TIME
Asparagus	2 bunches	Cut in half, trim stems	2 Tbsp	420°F	12-15 mins
Beets	1½ lbs	Peel, cut in ½-inch cubes	1Tbsp	390°F	28-30 mins
Bell peppers (for roasting)	4 peppers	Cut in quarters, remove seeds	1Tbsp	400°F	15-20 mins
Broccoli	1 large head	Cut in 1-2-inch florets	1Tbsp	400°F	15-20 mins
Brussels sprouts	1lb	Cut in half, remove stems	1Tbsp	425°F	15-20 mins
Carrots	1lb	Peel, cut in ¼-inch rounds	1 Tbsp	425°F	10-15 mins
Cauliflower	1 head	Cut in 1-2-inch florets	2 Tbsp	400°F	20-22 mins
Corn on the cob	7 ears	Whole ears, remove husks	1 Tbps	400°F	14-17 mins
Green beans	1 bag (12 oz)	Trim	1 Tbps	420°F	18-20 mins
Kale (for chips)	4 oz	Tear into pieces,remove stems	None	325°F	5-8 mins
Mushrooms	16 oz	Rinse, slice thinly	1 Tbps	390°F	25-30 mins
Potatoes, russet	1½ lbs	Cut in 1-inch wedges	1 Tbps	390°F	25-30 mins
Potatoes, russet	1lb	Hand-cut fries, soak 30 mins in cold water, then pat dry	½ -3 Tbps	400°F	25-28 mins
Potatoes, sweet	1lb	Hand-cut fries, soak 30 mins in cold water, then pat dry	1 Tbps	400°F	25-28 mins
Zucchini	1lb	Cut in eighths lengthwise, then cut in half	1 Tbps	400°F	15-20 mins

Beef

Item	Temp (°F)	Time (mins)	Item	Temp (°F)	Time (mins)
Beef Eye Round Roast (4 lbs.)	400 °F	45 to 55	Meatballs (1-inch)	370 °F	7
Burger Patty (4 oz.)	370 °F	16 to 20	Meatballs (3-inch)	380 °F	10
Filet Mignon (8 oz.)	400 °F	18	Ribeye, bone-in (1-inch, 8 oz)	400 °F	10 to 15
Flank Steak (1.5 lbs.)	400 °F	12	Sirloin steaks (1-inch, 12 oz)	400 °F	9 to 14
Flank Steak (2 lbs.)	400 °F	20 to 28			

Chicken

Item	Temp (°F)	Time (mins)	Item	Temp (°F)	Time (mins)
Breasts, bone in (1 ¼ lb.)	370 °F	25	Legs, bone-in (1 ¾ lb.)	380 °F	30
Breasts, boneless (4 oz)	380 °F	12	Thighs, boneless (1 ½ lb.)	380 °F	18 to 20
Drumsticks (2 ½ lb.)	370 °F	20	Wings (2 lb.)	400 °F	12
Game Hen (halved 2 lb.)	390 °F	20	Whole Chicken	360 °F	75
Thighs, bone-in (2 lb.)	380 °F	22	Tenders	360 °F	8 to 10

Pork & Lamb

Item	Temp (°F)	Time (mins)	Item	Temp (°F)	Time (mins)
Bacon (regular)	400 °F	5 to 7	Pork Tenderloin	370 °F	15
Bacon (thick cut)	400 °F	6 to 10	Sausages	380 °F	15
Pork Loin (2 lb.)	360 °F	55	Lamb Loin Chops (1-inch thick)	400 °F	8 to 12
Pork Chops, bone in (1-inch, 6.5 oz)	400 °F	12	Rack of Lamb (1.5 – 2 lb.)	380 °F	22

Fish & Seafood

Item	Temp (°F)	Time (mins)	Item	Temp (°F)	Time (mins)
Calamari (8 oz)	400 °F	4	Tuna Steak	400 °F	7 to 10
Fish Fillet (1-inch, 8 oz)	400 °F	10	Scallops	400 °F	5 to 7
Salmon, fillet (6 oz)	380 °F	12	Shrimp	400 °F	5
Swordfish steak	400 °F	10			

Index by Ingredients

Printed in Great Britain
by Amazon

74198295R00093